A HUNDRED YEARS OF JAPANESE LIFE IN HAWAII

KANYAKU IMIN

To King Kalalaua and all of the people of Hawaii who demonstrated and warmly conveyed their mutual love and respect to the Japanese arriving in Hawaii. This book is dedicated to furthering our efforts in keeping this spirit of aloha *alive.*

International Savings and Loan Association, Ltd.
National Mortgage Finance Company, Ltd.
Island Insurance Company, Ltd.
Mid-Pacific Television Associates (KHNL-TV)

Cover Photograph: Photographer unknown, from the Hawaii State Archives.

Frontispiece; Photographer unknown, from a logbook kept by the Waialua Sugar Plantation, Oahu, dated 1901.

Typography by Innovative Media Inc., Honolulu
Printed in Hong Kong by Toppan Printing Company (HK) Ltd
in cooperation with Emphasis International Ltd, Hong Kong,
Media Five Limited, Honolulu, and Michael Langley.
ISBN: 0-9615045-0-1

Inquiries should be directed to International Savings and Loan Association Ltd, 1111 Bishop Street, Honolulu, Hawaii 96813.

A HUNDRED YEARS OF JAPANESE LIFE IN HAWAII

KANYAKU IMIN

Edited and Produced by Leonard Lueras

Designed by Kunio Hayashi

With Editorial and Graphical Contributions by

Satoru Abe, Bumpei Akaji, Warren Bolster, Dan Boylan,
Reiko Mochinaga Brandon, Guy Buffet, O. A. Bushnell, Joe Carini,
Nedra Chung, Douglas Doi, Isami Doi, Dana Edmunds, Jocelyn Fujii, Deborah Boehm Gushman,
Jay Hartwell, Charles Higa, Randy Hokushin, Ron Hudson, Ihara, U.S. Sen. Daniel K. Inouye, Brian Isobe,
Val Kim, Tomi Kaizawa Knaefler, Marie Kodama, Paul Kodama, Akiko Kotani, Gaylord Kubota, David Kuraoka,
Michael Langley, Wayne Levin, Leonard Lueras, Mike Markrich, Mark Matsunaga, U.S. Sen. Spark Matsunaga,
Mary Mitsuda, Hiroki Morinoue, John Morita, Wayne Muromoto, Paul Nagano, Tetsuo Ochikubo,
Chris Pearce, Nina Hagiwara Peterson, Frank Salmoiraghi, Mamoru Sato, Tadashi Sato, Allan Seiden,
Naomi Sodetani, Toshiko Takaezu, Myles Tanaka, Usaku Teragawachi, Grady Timmons, Stan Tomita,
Corky Trinidad, Ray Tsuchiyama, Shuzo Uemoto, Brett Uprichard, Greg Vaughn,
Shige Yamada, Maile Yawata and Michael Young.

FIRST EDITION 1985

No	Names	Males	Females	Children	Employers		Advance	
✓ 326	Oki Hatsutaro				C+Co. Haiku	✓	9 -	
✓ 327	Kimura Risuke		1		C+Co Paia Planter	✓	9 -	
✓ 328	Watanuki Kanekichi				Kohala Sugar Co	✓	9 -	
✓ 329	Itamura Naojiro				C+Co. Paia Planter	✓	9 -	
✓ 330	Yamamoto Saro		1		C+Co. Haiku	✓	9 -	
✓ 331	Taone Tusajiro				C+C Haiku	✓	9 -	
✓ 332	Nishimmoto Harusaburo				C+Co. Paia Planter	✓	9 -	
✓ 333	Okino Rumejiro				C+Co. Paia Planter	✓	9 -	
✓ 334	Kamei Ginji		1		Faye & Meyer	✓ left blank	9/6	
✓ 335	Miki Tatsugora				Faye & Meyer	✓ " "	9/6	
✓ 336	Tudettshitaro				Faye & Meyer	✓	9/6	
✓ 337	Yamayguchi Kametaro		1		Faye & Meyer	✓ " "	9/6	
✓ 338	Goto Masuyora		1		Faye & Meyer	✓ " "	9/6	
✓ 339	Kato Tomizo				Faye & Meyer	✓ " "	9/6	
✓ 340	Iwaki Namige				Faye & Meyer	✓	9 -	
✓ 341	Kondt Nokaro				C. M. Cooke	✓ " "	9 -	
✓ 342	Seki Yasugoro				Faye & Meyer	✓ " "	9 -	
✓ 343	Katano Kitaro				Faye & Meyer	✓ " "	9 -	
✓ 344	Fukuda Sukejiro				Loper Wright Co	✓ " "	9 -	
✓ 345	Ichei Tatugoro				Faye & Meyer	✓ " "	9 -	
✓ 346	Nakayama Hangoro				Loper Wright Co.	✓ " "	9 -	
347	Mano Yoshimoto				R. W. Irwin ~~Faye & Meyer~~ ~~Loper Wright Co.~~	✓ (return to Japan)	9 -	
✓ 348	Kirie Kitaro				Faye & Meyer	✓ " "	9 -	
✓ 349	Yachima Tusajiro				Faye & Meyer	✓ " "	9 -	
✓ 350	Miyazaki Ichigoro				K K Co, & K Clarke	✓ " "	9 -	
✓ 351	Toda Yataro				Hakalau Sugar Co	✓ " "	9 -	
✓ 352	Kishimoto Shingoro				Hakalau Sugar Co	✓ " "	9/6	
							$ 291 -	

CONTENTS

On February 8, 1885, shortly after the first party of *Kanyaku Imin* had arrived in Hawaii on board the *City of Tokio* steamship, immigration officials signed the new contract laborers into a logbook (left) that identifies each worker, his or her sex, their plantation of destiny and the amount of money each received as an advance. Preceeding pages: Japanese workers who arrived later, in 1901, were individually photographed by their first Hawaii employer, Oahu's Waialua Sugar Company.

INTRODUCTION

Two paintings in my Washington, D.C., office serve as constant reminders of my childhood home on Queen Emma Street. The area of my youth was a crowded and chaotic mix of what planners labeled as slums. But I was much too young to realize how underprivileged I was and my parents were working so hard to preserve and protect our family that they had no time to worry about being poor. In this home there were no jangling conflicts between East and West, but rather a kind of stimulating blend of the two that characterizes the history of the Japanese community in Hawaii. When we ate chicken or beef, we used knives and forks. When we ate *sukiyaki* or *tempura*, we used chopsticks. Although I went to a Japanese school, it was never permitted to interfere with my American education.

Both my parents were raised with the Japanese language and I limped along in that tongue until I entered kindergarten, at which time my mother and father abruptly dropped Japanese and began to speak English — and only English — at home. Of course this was a hardship and a sacrifice and a great personal wrench for them, but they stuck painstakingly with it, perhaps the most striking demonstration of how far the Inouye family had traveled since my grandfather set out on the long road from Yokohama village just 25 years before. There would remain ties of tradition and sentiment with the old country, but there would never be any confusion about my parents' allegiance; they were Americans, a proud distillation of the union between the girl from Maui who had been raised a Methodist and the boy from Kauai whose forebears had been Buddhists.

This is not to say that either parent could or would summarily slam the door on their Japanese heritage. "I take from the old ways what I think is good and useful," my mother used to say. "I take from the new ways what is good and useful. Anyone would be foolish not to."

One of the old traditions was their reverence for the Emperor of Japan. I once asked my mother if a boy like me could ever aspire to marry his daughter. She did not consider the question at all foolish, but weighed it in all seriousness and at some length before answering me.

"Remember always," she finally said, "that there is no one who is too good for you." I felt myself grow taller. "But remember, too," she went on, "that there is a difference between pride and arro-

During his 1881 world tour, King Kalakaua met with the Emperor Meiji, who declined a marital alliance with the Hawaiian Kingdom. In this photo, King Kalakaua is flanked by Prince Fushimi and Joshii Tusentami, finance minister. Charles H. Judd, the king's chamberlain, stands in the back with Riyosuke Tokuno, first finance secretary; and William Armstrong, attorney general, on the right.

gance, for you are no better than anyone else, either."

Such were the personal recollections that flowed back to me when I was asked earlier this year to speak about the 100th Anniversary of the Japanese arrival in Hawaii. At this official kickoff of the Centennial Celebration in January, 1985, the words that I summoned were my own, but my thoughts were of individuals like my parents whose sacrifices and devotion enriched their children.

During the year-long observance of the 100th anniversary of the arrival of the pioneer contingent of Japanese immigrant contract workers much will be said and written about the great successes and achievements of the descendants of these brave pioneers and those who followed — stories of distinguished academicians and artists; of world-renowned physicians and scientists; of a governor and an astronaut; of Olympian gold medalists and war heroes; of U. S. senators, Congressmen and mayors; of outstanding leaders in business and labor; of movie stars and millionaires; and many, many more. These success stories are real, they are exciting and dramatic, and worthy of public recitation, but they may be told and retold to the point where some may lose sight of the significance, the bravery and the sacrifices of the early immigrant field workers. Lest we forget, may I respectfully suggest that though today's generations of descendants may represent thousands of inspiring success stories, we succeeded because of a priceless legacy which we inherited from these early immigrants. This legacy was not of material wealth or vast estates — they were poor contract laborers and illiteracy was commonplace. Very few were eloquent in language or articulate in expression — but by their simple and easily forgotten deeds, they taught us the importance of human values. This was their legacy.

— Daniel K. Inouye, U.S. Senator

What is earned at great price is treasured the most. This truth is reflected in the American experience of those of Japanese ancestry in Hawaii, as it has been for so many others in this great immigrant nation of ours founded on ideals of human freedom and dignity, rather than on a prevailing blood line.

As a *nisei*, I value my Japanese "roots," which have taken hold in a special place within the United States, where many races have been privileged to share in the rich heritage and surroundings of the Hawaiians. Would that all of us, of all ancestries, had returned the hospitality King Kalakaua, and his people, accorded our immigrant forebears a century ago! My father, Kingoro, had ventured to Hawaii to escape the rigors of life in a monastery in Japan to which his father had sent him for priesthood training. When he met my mother, Chiyono (Fukushima) Ikeda, she was a widowed picture bride with four children. Their own union produced three more of us; I was my father's first son, my mother's fifth child. At that time, the sugar plantation at Kukuiula, Kauai, where father labored, paid only a dollar a day. With seven children, even with my mother operating a family *tofu* factory with the youngest child strapped to her back, my father couldn't make ends meet.

Despite our poverty, my father imparted a strict ethical code on his offspring. He placed great stress on honesty. We were never to steal or beg. At times when the children would receive food from kindly friends, he would angrily reprimand us for behaving like a *"kojiki"* (a lowly despicable beggar) and force us to return it.

As a youngster, I failed fully to appreciate the justice of laboring in the family *tofu* factory, while my peers were out playing ball. We were also required to gather firewood for the camp *furo* that father operated in Kukuiula. Whenever I gathered enough courage to voice my complaints, my father admonished me with an ancient Japanese adage, *"Kuro ga atte fukai jinsei ga wakaru* (Personal suffering leads to better understanding of human values)."

Four years after finishing high school while working as a sales clerk and bookkeeper at Mikado Store in Hanapepe I had the good fortune of winning a newspaper subscription sales contest and the princely cash prize of $1,000. In keeping with the Japanese tradition of *"oya-koko,"* (filial piety), I presented $600 of the prize money to my parents, bought them their first electric refrigerator, and begged them to let me enter the University of Hawaii in Honolulu. I was the first of my family to do so, and left Kauai, entrusting a flock of chickens I was raising to my mother's care.

Another four years later, in 1941, when I was awarded my degree, my brothers and sisters presented my parents with the funds necessary to travel to Honolulu to attend my graduation. It was the most emotion-laden moment of my life, when my mother came up to me after the graduation ceremony, as I proudly stood in the cap and gown of a newly-minted bachelor of education, and presented to me my graduation gift — it was a bank passbook showing a $2,000 balance! She had deposited into my account the earnings of my chickens from egg sales and every penny I had been sending her regularly from my part-time job wages, compounded with interest over the period I had been away.

Soon after graduation I was to experience the call to battle in World War II, when the loyalty of Americans of Japanese ancestry was to be validated in blood and lives overseas, even as it was being questioned behind barbed-wire fences at home. The aftermath of that strange time of strife, when our country's ideals were at once heightened by national resolve and fell short by human inconsistency, was to add new maturity and luster to the realization of the American dream.

But for me, on that graduation day with the future ahead of me, I basked in my ethnic inheritance from my parents and siblings, a family's priceless *aloha*!

— Spark M. Matsunaga, U.S. Senator

'TENJIKU' TODAY

The gods brought them safely across the wide waters, to the promised land. On the thirtieth day of their voyaging they saw many birds flying about, skimming the sea for food, and, towering above the horizon to the southeast, great masses of clouds. 'Land is near,' the sailors said, pointing toward the clouds, and the eager passengers gathered on deck to catch their first glimpse of it. Later in the afternoon they were rewarded: the clouds drew apart and floated away, and the people saw, green and golden in the slanting light, the rampart mountains of Kauai, lifted high above the sea. 'There is Tenjiku,' they said. 'It is not a vision. It is a paradise . . .'

" . . . The best part about arriving in Tenjiku, they agreed, was the fact that it brought them nearer to the time when they would begin to work for those rich sugar planters. Thoughts of all the honorable money they were going to earn, visions of all the estimable gold they would save and all the respect they would receive when they returned home comforted them for the hardships they had endured during the voyage, strengthened them for the work that lay ahead. The discovery that this place was not really like the Lord Buddha's Tenjiku did not dismay them. Paradise must wait. In this world a man must do the best he can, to bear the life the gods have arranged for him . . . "

—Author O. A. Bushnell, writing about the *Gannenmono,* or First Year Men, who immigrated to Hawaii from Japan in 1868. From *The Stone of Kannon,* 1979.

Mrs. Hatsu Kimura left for Hawaii with her husband Shichigoro on April 28, 1907. Fourteen days later, she presented her passport (at left) in Honolulu. The Kimuras hoped to make their fortune and return to Japan. They never went back. Preceding pages: the rich coffee hills of Kona enticed free and escaped sugar plantation laborers, and many of their third generation children still work there.

Taro fields covered Waipio Valley on the Big Island in the 1700s when it was home for thousands of Hawaiians. The seductions of civilization and later a tidal wave almost wiped out the settlement. Today, Tom Arakaki and a few others farm the starchy root that's mashed into edible *poi*. At right: Japanese laborers left the plantations for the cities or homesteads, where coffee, orchids and these anthuriums now grow.

16

A coffee farmer carries his beans past a Kona drying shed. At left: for 34 years, Mrs. Sumiye Aoki operated a sewing shop in Haleiwa. In 1981 she retired and with her son Michael transformed the shop into Aoki's Shave Ice. Following pages: many Japanese adopted the customs of their new home — including the Hawaiian's *hula*.

At the Waikoloa Rodeo on the Big Island, *paniolo* Alvin Kawamoto ropes a cow. At left: Kalani High graduate Tom Nishimura got a mechanical engineering degree from the University of Hawaii and now he's designing sails for his own windsurfing company, Vortech. His "foot batten surf sail" helps him jump over this wave.

Japan's sport of sumo attracted Hawaii-born Jesse "Takamiyama" Kuhaulua (at left) and Salevaa "Konishiki" Atisanoe—neither of whom are Japanese. Takasago Oyakata, the stablemaster who coached Takamiyama to his championships, reads a message of congratulation to Jesse during his 1984 retirement ceremony in Honolulu. At right: the Japanese veterans of America's 442nd Regimental Combat Team honored Takamiyama with this *keshomawashi,* a ceremonial loin cloth worn by *sumotori.* The 442nd's "Go For Broke" motto capsulizes the career of Jesse, the first foreigner to win Japan's much coveted and prestigious Emperor's Cup.

Japanese field workers of the Hawaiian Commercial & Sugar Company sat for this portrait in 1913 at the Kawano Photo Studio, Puunene, Maui. At right: this Japanese couple posed in 1895 for Christian J. Hedemann in Honolulu. The *kimono*-dressed woman maintains the traditions of Japan, standing behind her husband with her hand on his shoulder.

GANNENMONO AND KANYAKU IMIN

Prior to 1885 and the official blessing of King Kalakaua, Japanese people were a minor part of Hawaii's immigrant population. A few Japanese survivors of shipwrecks arrived in the Islands as early as 1806, but neither they nor subsequent shipwrecked Japanese stayed long. Indeed, it wasn't until June 19, 1868, that a Japanese group of any size arrived in Hawaii from the Land of the Rising Sun. On that date, a British sailing ship, HMS *Scioto,* put into Honolulu with the Islands' first immigrant workers from Japan—148 men and five women. These "Gannen-mono," or First Year Men as they were known (they came to Hawaii during the first year of the Meiji Emperor's reign), were quickly assimilated into the plantation labor force, earning 12½ cents a day, or, according to one account, "about twice what they could make in Japan." By 1885 their wage had quadrupled to about 50 cents a day, or about $15 per month, but tight immigration laws under the Kamehameha and Lunalilo governments made it almost impossible for Japanese workers to enter the Hawaiian Kingdom. Also the Japanese government expressed its concern about how the Gannen-mono had been treated by their Hawaii plantation employers. Then came Kalakaua—the patron king of the Japanese in Hawaii.

Kalakaua, more than anybody else in Hawaii's history, made it possible for large numbers of Japanese to immigrate to his beautiful land. Consequently, Japanese are now the second largest racial-ethnic group in the Islands, following the Caucasians. The Japanese in Hawaii also have attained positions of power in the Islands. Among other accomplishments, island residents of Japanese descent include two U.S. senators, the governor of Hawaii and the mayor of Kauai.

In one way or another, all these *issei, nisei, sansei, yonsei* and *gosei* children of Nippon can thank the Merrie Monarch, Kalakaua, for their fortune. At the very least they can recall the gracious and sportive way in which the first group of Japanese contract laborers, the original *Kanyaku Imin,* were

Two years after their 1868 arrival in Hawaii, 43 of the original, 153 *Gannenmono* returned to Japan, unhappy with the Islands' working conditions. One who stayed married a Hawaiian and produced these *hapa* children. Following page: plantation workers flume cane at the Paia, Maui, sugar plantation in 1920.

personally greeted by the King, and how they, in turn, expressed their thankfulness.

About four years earlier, in March 1981, Kalakaua, on a world tour stopover in Tokyo, and his attorney general, W. N. Armstrong, initiated treaty discussions with Japan. Among the major considerations was Japanese immigration to Hawaii. As historian Ralph Kuykendall notes in his book *The Hawaiian Kingdom, 1874–1893,* "The king let it be known that, in accordance with the policy of the government of Hawaii to increase population by inviting immigration from other countries, any Japanese who desired to settle in the Hawaiian kingdom would be permitted to do so."

Kalakaua was keen to establish good relations with Japan, and he even went to the diplomatic extreme of proposing to the Meiji emperor that the 15-year-old Crown Prince Hatsu become betrothed to Princess Kaiulani, his six-year-old *hapa-haole* niece who was a direct heir to his throne. And "to the emperor privately," Kuykendall reports, "Kalakaua suggested the formation of a federation of Asiatic nations, of which the Japanese ruler would be the head and Hawaii would be one of the member nations."

The marriage and Asiatic federation schemes never materialized, but Kalakaua's Hawaiian government actively pursued Japanese immigration. Such a move eventually was given official sanction and funding by both governments, and on February 8, 1885 a first group of 943 Japanese immigrants—676 men, 159 women and 108 children—arrived in Honolulu on board a Pacific Mail steamer, the *City of Tokio.* The *Pacific Commercial Advertiser* described the arrival of the first Japanese contract laborers, the *Kanyaku Imin,* "as the most important event that has happened in Hawaii for many years.'

Under Kalakaua's direction the Hawaiian Kingdom rolled out a rainbow carpet for the Japanese. The Royal Hawaiian Band played music for them, Honolulu policemen served as tour guides, and all necessary food, shelter and medical needs were provided. Three days after their arrival, the Japanese repaid the King's *aloha* with a special sports exhibition in honor of the eleventh anniversary celebration of Kalakaua's accession to the Hawaiian throne (see pgs. 32–33).

On March 11, 1885, Japan's then Consul General in Hawaii, Jiro Nakamura, reported to his government that, "The signing of labor contracts between our voluntary emigrants and the President of the Bureau of Immigration has been completed and job placements have been concluded. Our people started to leave for their respective job sites on the 16th of last month and all had left by the 23rd. It is still too premature to make a detailed report on working conditions, but as reported earlier, our people are being treated very kindly by the people of Hawaii. . . ."

—Leonard Lueras

"Yesterday afternoon the Japanese at the Immigration Depot had an exhibition of wrestling that was very interesting and amusing.

"His Majesty the King was invited to be present, and witnessed the sports from the music stand. He was accompanied by his Chamberlain, Col. C. H. Judd, and there was also present their excellencies the Premier and the Attorney-General, the United States Minister and his wife, Honorable A. S. Cleghorn, L. McCully and Mrs. McCully, Col. Iaukea and Mrs. Iaukea, General Van Buren, Prof. Scott and Mrs. Scott, Hon. John Cummins and others, who thoroughly enjoyed the sport.

"Consul-General Irwin was busied in giving directions to the representatives of the various provinces, and when His Majesty arrived the people were presented to him en masse.

"The ring or arena in which the wrestling took place was within one of the grassy courts, and was prepared by encircling a sanded space with bags filled with sand so as to form a wrestling ground about 12 feet in diameter. Previous to the commencement of the games a small mound of sand was piled up in the center of the space, and in this was planted a staff decked with fluttering streamers of white paper. At one side, a little back from the ring was piled up some ten tubs of "sahkee," a favorite Japanese drink. These were to be the prizes awarded to the successful party in the approaching match. On the opposite side of the ring was a seat covered with a scarlet blanket, on which was seated three women with 3-stringed banjos, which they twanged as an accompaniment to a preliminary chorus.

"On three sides of the square, within which was the ring, the Japanese gathered as thick as bees, while the innate politeness that is part of the religion of this peculiar people, the women were given seats on the grass in front of the men.

"The contestants in the wrestling match were divided into parties of about 20 men each. They were designated as the "East" and "West" and took opposite sides of the sandy arena. Four bamboos were planted around the other edge of the ring, and buckets of water and tins filled with rice flour were placed in readiness. Those who were to take part in the wrestling wore nothing but a band of cloth passed between their legs and then wound around the waist. Their naked bodies showed every degree of muscular development, some being without any superfluous flesh, but with plenty of sinew, while others were clothed with an abundance of solid brawn, and a few were inclined to fatness. They were all amateur wrestlers, there being no "professionals" engaged.

"All things being in readiness the manager stepped forward with his fan of office, and announced the beginning of the sport. At a signal, two men stepped on to the sanded surface (that had been carefully leveled off) and after a few feints came together with a rush, grasped each other by the waist cloth, and after a brief, sharp struggle, came to the ground together, one being on top. He, being the victor, sprang immediately to his feet in time to meet a fresh man from the party to which the defeated one belonged, and, in his turn was thrown. A loud roar of applause from the West announced the fact that their side was even again, and then

two others stepped forward. They squatted opposite each other for a moment, rubbing their sanded hands together, and then commenced sparring for a good hold. The play of their open hands was very rapid, and at least one ducked, ran his head into the other's chest, flung his arm over his opponent's back, seized his waist band, and had him down in an instant. Quick as thought he was on the defensive again, and tried to repeat the trick with the next man. He failed, however, and was run backwards out of the ring, which was equivalent to a defeat.

"His conqueror had no time to spare, for a rival met him as he turned, and for a moment or two the sand flew about quite lively. Finally, in some mysterious way, he was thrown off his balance and brought to his knees — a proceeding which was hailed with loud shouts of applause from the East.

"The umpire, who alone remained in the ring with the wrestlers, stepped forward each time a man was downed, and with a wave of his fan announced the result. Only once was there any occasion for anyone else to interfere, and that was when a victor was attacked a little too suddenly from behind by a fresh combatant. Then the men from each side rushed in, each one vociferating at the top of his voice, and for a moment there was nothing to be seen but a struggling mass of men packed closely together like brokers on the floor of a stock exchange — only the Japs behaved better. The head men rushed in, the band struck up a lively air, and in a minute the noisy crowd divided the two parties squatted down again, and the wrestling went on.

"There was every variety of clutch,

hold, slip, trip and feint employed, and men were run or pitched headlong out of the ring; thrown with gentle violence (one of them broke a stout wooden pail when he came down on it), or dexterously pulled down on their faces. Roars of laughter greeted the defeat of some and loud applause the skillful feats of others. All the wrestlers displayed the utmost good nature, grinning good humoredly at defeat or victory.

"After about an hour's exhibition of their skill and muscle, the umpire declared the wrestling finished, and the victory was awarded to the East. In what mysterious way the question was decided no one outside of the ring could possibly determine, but all seemed satisfied.

"Thereupon ensued a sort of dance of triumph by the leading ones in the East. Fastening around their waists red, yellow and blue blankets (in imitation of the gorgeous silk wrapping which Consul Irwin informs us the professionals wear on such occasions), they commenced a slow, stately ring dance; chanting and gesticulating after the manner of the Gilbert Islanders, or the mount Lebanon Quakers perhaps. They sang their valorous deeds, and indulged in a few jokes at the expense of the West, who grinned their appreciation of the fun. Then the piled up tubs of sahke were approached, and the top one being taken down (it was about 18 inches in diameter, and 2 feet high), it was seized and tossed aloft by as many as could possibly get hold of it. It reminded some present of the Gothic ceremony of heaving aloft a victorious chief on a shield. Finally the tub was set upon the ground, the head broken in, and all crowded forward for a deep draught of the liquor.

"While the people were thus engaged, Consul Irwin invited his guests on the music platform to taste of the same liquor, and all pronounced it genuine — sahke. It isn't cat-lap at any rate. Some boxes of Japanese snap biscuits were opened and scattered amongst the crowd, who seemed to highly appreciate the goodies.

"The wrestling match was preceded by a fencing match called Gekkin. The two combatants were armed with two-handled, straight wooden swords about 5 feet long. Their heads were defended by heavy helmets, the faces being covered by a wire mask. The hands were protected by padded gloves, breast plates and greaves were worn, and thus protected they went at each other quite scientifically. The attack and defence was very good, one or the other now and then acknowledging a cut or thrust. The performance was followed by some acrobatic feats on an upright ladder, and then came the wrestling described above.

"Finally, a grave-looking party mounted on a tub in the middle of the ring, and, hoisting a fish-skin umbrella over his head, commenced a song which another man accompanied by taps on one of the drums borrowed from the band. Surrounding the singer was a ring of people, who came in on chorus.

"This wound up the day's sports, with which all expressed themselves very much pleased. The remark was made that such people on a plantation would help to make things lively, and there certainly was a fine display of muscle, pluck and good nature . . ."

—From the February 12, 1885 issue of *The Pacific Commercial Advertiser*

"**Sumo wrestlers** entertain the royal court," a painting by Guy Buffet.

In 1917, picture bride Osame Manago and her husband Kinzo (in wedding portrait) opened the Manago Hotel in Captain Cook, Hawaii, with $100 borrowed from a plantation boss. Their grandson Dwight runs the hotel today. At left: Steere Noda was once a member of Hawaii's first Japanese baseball team, the Asahi.

Among the treasured memorabilia of *kamaaina* families of any ethnic background one will invariably find "old-fashioned" family studio portraits, many of which have begun to show signs of their age in the fading and other blemishing of their precious images. What few people realize is that if the photos were taken in the islands during the first half of this century the odds are overwhelming that on the other side of the camera was a Japanese photographer. Individuals may recall that "oh yeah, there was a Japanese man who used to take our picture;" what they are not in a position to realize is that the story was the same for family after family in town after town throughout the islands.

Five years ago a Bishop Museum exhibition and companion publication, *Na Pa'i Ki'i: The Photographers in the Hawaiian Islands, 1845–1900*, documented and stunningly presented the pioneering role of professional and amateur Caucasian photographers in Hawaii up to the turn of the century. By 1900, however, Japanese immigrants were already playing a very significant role in commercial photography. Within a decade they would almost completely dominate the field.

These early *shashinya-san* were also pioneers of photography. Their major contribution to the technological and social history of Hawaii lay in introducing photography to outlying areas and plantation towns. A guide to Japanese businesses in Hawaii published in 1909 listed 58 photographers widely distributed throughout the islands. Their distribution is a reminder of how Hawaii's population was once centered on numerous plantation towns, many of which are now gone.

The Big Island had 27 *shashinya-san*, nearly twice as many as any other island. These included four in Hilo, two in Hawi, two in Olaa and six in the large Kona district; the remaining *shashinya-san* were scattered among 13 plantation towns. Oahu had 15, half of whom were in Honolulu. Kauai, with two each in Hanapepe and Koloa, and Maui, with three in Lahaina and two in Wailuku, each had a total of eight.

The English-language directory for Hawaii for 1909 listed only seven non-Japanese photographers: three Chinese, one Portuguese and three other Caucasians. By 1909, therefore, nearly 90 percent of the commercial photographers in Hawaii were Japanese. Who were these photographers, when did they get started in Hawaii, and how did they learn their profession?

The earliest Japanese photographers whose arrival in Hawaii can be documented in Honolulu Japanese Consulate and Hawaii State Archives records, Rinpei (R.P. in English-language directories) Sumida and Katsujiro Hamamoto, came as plantation contract laborers. Sumida arrived in February 1886 on the "Third Ship" of Government Contract Japanese immigrants. His three-year contract began on February 16th and his monthly wage was $9 plus a $6 food allowance. Hamamoto arrived late the following year and was sent to Koloa Plantation on Kauai. Whether they brought photographic skills with them or acquired them in Hawaii is uncertain.

At least a few of the early *shashinya-san* clearly came as photographers rather than as laborers. The arrival of K. Amaya in February 1894 was even noted in the *Hawaiian Gazette*: "Amaya, a Japanese artist and photographer, arrived in steerage from Yokohama. . . An attaché of the Japanese Legation stated yesterday that Amaya ranks very high in his profession in Japan." The following month Minetaro Shirai arrived and opened a studio on Kauai. Yoshio Yamamoto, who arrived in late 1898, was reportedly a highly-trained artist. After opening an art gallery in Honolulu he discovered that there was a far greater demand for his services as a photographer and pursued that as a career until he eventually retired and returned to Japan.

On the other hand, it is equally clear that others learned photography in Hawaii. Ryunosuke Susumago operated a studio in Hilo in the mid-1890s and shifted his place of business to Honolulu shortly before the turn of the century. The late Charlotte Susumago, Ryunosuke's daughter-in-law, recalled her husband saying that his father was not trained for any profession but had artistic talent. He got into photography through retouching negatives for a photographer.

Most of the subsequent *shashinya-san* received their training by working and studying at the studios of their well-established predecessors from Japan. A close look at the biographical sketches of 16 photographers included in a 1927 directory of Japanese in Hawaii makes this very clear. These men had come to Hawaii between 1899 and 1920, with most arriving between 1906 and 1912. Eleven acknowledged learning or improving their photographic skills at established studios, and only one of them did so at the studio of a *gaijin* (non-Japanese). Four had spent at least some time at the studio of Yoshio Yamamoto. Only one of the 16, Wataru Shimizu, whose father Torao was also a photographer, attended a Mainland photography school.

Not only did they learn from the old-timers, but in a number of instances they bought the studios of those who returned to Japan or retired. The late Shigeki Hayashi (William S. Hayashi), father-in-law of Governor George Ariyoshi, is an example of a "late-comer" who trained under an old-timer and later bought the studio of another old-timer. Dislike of harsh field work at Ewa Plantation led young Hayashi, who was only 16 when he arrived in Hawaii in 1912, to become an apprentice at Katsujiro Hamamoto's Pacific Photo Studio. In 1917 Hayashi opened his own studio on King Street near Aala Park. It was a classic, walk-up studio on the second floor, and on Saturdays Filipino plantation workers who had arrived in town at the nearby Oahu Railway Depot lined the stairway to have their photos taken. Hayashi would retouch the photos to improve them for the folks back home, particularly if a photo might be used in the search for a prospective bride. He was also one of the first photographers here to use a three-color dye process to create experimental color images. His studio was so prosperous that after a few years he was able to buy out Yoshio Yamamoto's establishment at the corner of King and Nuuanu when Yamamoto returned to Japan after a quarter of a century as the leading Japanese photographer in Hawaii.

Because most towns had only one photographer, the early Japanese photographers recorded all important occasions—such as weddings, births and deaths—and made it possible for immigrants of all nationalities to send photos back to their homelands as well as to leave behind the photos now treasured by their descendents in Hawaii. Because cameras for snapshot photography were not readily available or affordable in the early days, formal portraits taken by the early Japanese commercial photographers are the only images that many in Hawaii have of their immigrant ancestors. Theirs is a legacy for us all.

—Gaylord Kubota

On Boy's Day in Olaa, Hawaii, about 1915, the carp were hung.

The Last Picture Bride

When 19-year-old Tama Teramoto left Japan for Hawaii in June of 1923, she had no idea she was about to become a footnote to history. Ever since a Gentleman's Agreement of 1905, the flow of Japanese immigrants coming to the Islands had slowed—but so-called "picture brides" were still being admitted. Under new immigration laws, Tama Teramoto was to be the last.

Tama knew next to nothing about Susumu Nishimura of Lanai. They had exchanged pictures and that was all. The marriage had been arranged by their respective parents.

A farmer's daughter, Tama came from Kumamoto, a prefecture known for its rough dialect and hard-headed people. Before she left, her parents gave her a small bag of earth which had been blessed at the local Shinto shrine.

With that bag of earth in hand, she boarded the ship *Korea Maru* in Nagasaki. Traveling third class, she went first to Kobe and then to Yokohama before setting sail for Hawaii.

"When I left people were saying, 'Hawaii, Hawaii'," she remembers. "But where was this Hawaii they were talking about? I didn't really know. At that time, 61 years ago, when my parents told me to do something, I did it without question."

The *Korea Maru* docked in Honolulu Harbor on June 26, 1923, eight days after leaving Yokohama. Tama was one of nine picture brides on board, but the last to leave the immigration depot. Long after the other picture brides had been taken, Tama waited. It would be another week before Susumu came for her. When the news reached Lanai that his bride had arrived, he didn't care to go and meet her. He told his father, "Well, you're the one who ordered her.

You go." When Susumu and his father finally showed up, Tama was overcome with relief. "My, you come at last!" she said.

After a 24-hour acquaintance period, the two were married at Izumo Taisha, a Shinto shrine in downtown Honolulu. They boarded a schooner for Lahaina, Maui, and from there took a small motor boat across the channel to Lanai.

One wonders what Tama's thoughts were as she was being taken to her new home. Here she sat in the back of a small boat, crossing open ocean to a location that was becoming more and more remote. "My attitude was, anyplace will do as long as there is work," she says. "And there was work to do on Lanai."

Lanai at that time was a dry, barren plain. The Dole Pineapple Company had yet to turn the island into the giant pineapple plantation that it is today. Most of the population, which numbered fewer than 100, worked as cattle ranchers and cowboys for the Koele Ranch.

Tama's new life was not an easy one. Within a month after her arrival, the wife of Susumu's father ran away—"she must have been waiting for me to come," Tama says—leaving Tama to care for Susumu's father, four brothers and sister.

A year after she arrived, the first of her three daughters was born, and her duties seemed to double. Her second year on Lanai she gave birth to her only son, but he lived less than a week.

During the day, Tama worked at Koele Ranch. Lanai was full of surveyors who were laying out the present-day Lanai City, and at the boarding house Tama made butter, hand-laun-

dered clothes and worked as a waitress. She served breakfast, lunch and dinner, and then she would come home, don her *kimono* and *obi* and serve dinner for her husband's family as well.

She earned a dollar a day, but the money went to support her husband's family. Any money that was left over was to be saved to send Susumu's father back to Japan.

She longed for Japan herself. Her most tangible tie to the homeland was the little bag of earth her parents had given her. She still had it, having carefully placed it in a small Shinto arrangement in her new home.

Tama found her husband to be a remarkable man. Susumu had grown up in Hawaii, among Hawaiian people, and had moved from Maui to Lanai when he was 11. He was a gifted story teller. He spoke Hawaiian fluently, as well as English and the rough Kumamoto dialect. At various times, he worked as a mail carrier, a carpenter, an electrician, a mechanic, a theater manager and a member of the provisional police.

Tama used to love to tell the story of how he made enough money to send his father back to Japan. Miyoko, her second daughter, remembers it well: "Many years ago, a man came from Maui with a car," she says. "He was here for about a month and decided he didn't like it. So here was this car. On a moment's notice, Susumu went and borrowed the $400 to buy it. And when he drove it home, his father gave him the scolding of his life. *How are you going to pay for this thing?* But, you know, there was nothing to do on Lanai at night. The men would all go down to the harbor—to a place called Miki

Camp — and drink and gamble until morning.

"Susumu realized they had no way, so he began a taxi service. The car had a little running board on the side, and if it was full the men stood on the running board. If they couldn't pay, he said, 'That's okay, next time.' And they would remember. They'd get half drunk playing cards, and give him enormous tips. The family often waited up for him, and at two or three o'clock in the morning he would come in, lay the money on the table and they would count. He paid for the car in a week. And soon he had enough money to send his father back to Japan."

About a week after his father left, a fire broke out in the garage where Susumu parked his car. "When he saw the rubble he was in shock because here was this car that had been earning him so much money!" says Miyoko. "But he found a few of the engine parts and realized maybe he should try to put it back together. And that's how he became a mechanic."

That was also the beginning of the Nishimura Service Station, which became the only service station on Lanai and the family's source of income for many years.

In 1968, more than 50 years after she came to Lanai, Tama Nishimura made her first and only trip back to Japan. She visited Kumamoto province where her younger brother was now Governor. She went to the Shinto shrine in the village where she was born and raised. She had a small gift she wanted to give the priest. It was the bag of earth she had kept all these years. Now it was time to put it back in the ground.

— Grady Timmons

39

The Benshi: On Making People Weep

His popularity was extreme and was based on that very quality which had made films so instantly popular: Japanese enthusiasm for self-improvement. Then as now the Japanese were unfailingly curious and, at the same time, unfailingly disturbed lest they not understand everything. This audience created the *benshi*, gave him enormous prestige, and paid him his not inconsiderable rewards . . . His effect on the Japanese film is almost impossible to overestimate . . ."
— from the book *Japanese Cinema* by Donald Richie

Benshi. The word refers to a story teller. But for the first half of this century a *benshi* was one who voiced character parts and provided the narration behind silent Japanese cinema.

For a homesick immigrant culture, films were not mere entertainment. They were a vicarious trip back, a powerful reminder of home. "The movies taught certain Japanese moral precepts, such as to honor one's parents," says ninety-year-old Kamesuke Nakahama, one of Honolulu's three surviving *benshi*. "Through this process, the audience would reaffirm being Japanese. It was the weepies, the melodramas, that were the most popular. It wasn't a good movie unless the audience cried and all eyes turned red. Only then did they feel they had seen a good film. Perhaps when they emerged from the theater, their own lives didn't seem so bad."

Nakahama's career as a *benshi* began in 1923 at the age of 28 — and lasted 28 years. Born in the prefecture

The benshi beams (above). Right: a scene from a Japanese silent film, *Father*, 1924.

40

of Yamaguchi, he came to Hawaii at the age of 17 when his father sent for him. He dreamed of being an actor, but on the island of Maui the opportunities were few indeed. When a theater operator there suggested he try being a *benshi,* Nakahama realized his chance.

To his surprise, his first performance was a great success, and word of his talent soon spread. One night a man from a big Honolulu theater was in the audience and afterwards asked him to return with him. "It was a turn of fate that changed my life forever," says Nakahama. "If I hadn't been discovered that night, I might have ended my life on Maui as a nobody."

In his new career as a *benshi,* Nakahama kept a grueling schedule. He worked seven days a week and did eight shows on Sunday. Surely he grew bored of seeing the same film so many times? "Oh, no," he says. "My rhythm and timing got better with each performance, so I actually enjoyed it more."

Nakahama viewed a show at least four times before trying it out on an audience. During a performance, he sat in a corner to the right of the screen with a microphone but no reading light. He wore a *montsuki,* a black cape-like garb with sharp, angular shoulders that he put on over a *kimono.* He voiced the titles as they appeared on the screen, and in between provided a narration that was often of his own construction. The timing and wording of the narration were crucial. "The trick when explaining the narrative was to keep it as simple as possible," he says. "Otherwise, you lose your audience."

At the height of silent Japanese cinema, Nakahama says there were about

15 *benshi* in Honolulu. Usually they were tied to a specific theater, which was tied to a specific film company in Japan. When a film went to the Neighbor Islands, the *benshi* often went along as a sort of traveling soundtrack. On these occasions, he did the show alone. For his Honolulu performances he had a helper, or *bansho,* who recorded sound effects and played them back at the appropriate moments during the film. *Bansho* were usually women or others in the performing arts who also played traditional Japanese instruments such as the *samisen, koto* and *shakuhachi.*

When World War II came, the *benshi* found themselves out of work. All Japanese movie houses in Honolulu closed down, and Japanese films were destroyed or sold in Asia. Nakahama took a job in a restaurant. When the war was over, so too was the era of the silent film.

"In 1946 I was approached to do a show for old times sake," Nakahama says. "I said, 'No, I already have a job,'

But they persisted and I gave in. When they brought me back, the lines were unbelievable to see the *benshi* again."

Although the coming of sound ended one career, Nakahama soon found a new one. He became head of promotions for the Kokusai Theater, escorting Japanese movie stars around when they visited Hawaii.

In recent years, he has been called on to give performances at the Kennedy Theater on the University of Hawaii campus and at Honolulu's annual East-West Film Festival.

But it is among his contemporaries that he remains most popular. "At senior citizen gatherings, people still come up to me and say, 'Nakahama-san, when will you do one of your shows for us? Only you can make us weep and cry.' Many of these people, like myself, think this was the best time in their life. They want to see the silent movie and hear the *benshi* to recall those great moments again."

— Grady Timmons

42

WORLDS REDISCOVERED

The year is 1981, and in downtown Honolulu two workers renovating an aging Hotel Street building have discovered piles of dusty, cobwebbed glass plates. They hold one up to the bright sun and they see a beautiful old image of a formal sitting portrait. Eventually, more than 4,000 of these glass negatives were donated to the Bishop Museum, and the museum's archivists began to trace the origin of these unknown photographs. Like the unearthing of other human historical treasures that reveal the richness of daily life in long-forgotten cultures, these mysterious glass plates presented—frame by frame—a detailed look at Honolulu's flourishing Japanese community from the beginning of World War I to the Great Depression. The collection was ultimately attributed to Usaku Teragawachi, perhaps one of the best portrait photographers in Hawaii during this century.

Born in the 21st year of the Meiji Reign (1889) in Yamaguchi Prefecture in southern Japan, Usaku Teragawachi arrived in Hawaii in 1906 as a contract laborer assigned to the Big Island's Hakalau sugar plantation. When his contract expired, Teragawachi left for Hilo, where he most likely worked as an apprentice for a photographer. In 1913 he established the Art Photograph Gallery in downtown Honolulu at 20 Hotel Street, a few buildings down from On Char's City Photo Company, another landmark portrait establishment.

Though Teragawachi began to cater to an almost exclusively Japanese clientele, his society was comprised of sharp contrasts. Although the first airplane flight in Hawaii had been completed three years before Teragawachi's studio opened, some Hawaiians still lived in grass shacks, and the Hawaiian monarchy was faintly alive.

In a sense, to "read" a photograph is to probe deeply into a lost world. Teragawachi's portraits show an immigrant culture in fast transition from feudal origins to Westernization. The Japanese

The striking Usaku Teragawachi images reproduced on these pages (42 to 53) are but a tiny sampler of thousands of Teragawachi images presently being printed and curated by the Bernice Pauahi Bishop Museum. Each glass-plate image, however, boldly and sensitively shows off Teragawachi's masterful use of natural studio light.

community, which would grow over the next few decades to nearly 40 percent of Hawaii's population, was a complex mixture of picture brides from Japan's southern farming regions, flappers wearing new *Vogue* designs from Paris, *nouveau riche* shopkeepers and veterans of the Great War. Instead of the traditional vision of all Japanese immigrants as plantation workers in a harsh environment, their portraits show a people urbanized, entrepreneurial and, most remarkable of all, at ease in their new environment.

Teragawachi's Art Photograph Gallery was aptly-named, since his photographic work was a lifelong artistic pursuit. Instead of Ray Jerome Baker's romantic images of native Hawaiian life, or the photojournalism of Tai Sing Loo, Teragawachi was a classical portrait photographer. One can imagine the ever-meticulous Teragawachi, quietly hovering over his bulky camera before customers posed in front of an Edwardian backdrop. On some occasions, Teragawachi would leave his downtown studio to photograph funeral processions, religious ceremonies, or families posed alongside their new possessions. Later in his career, Teragawachi specialized in "hand-painting" colorful patterns on *kimonos* for wedding portraits and Cherry Blossom Queen contestants — a unique genre somewhere in-between photography and painting. He did such documenting almost up to his death in 1964.

For Hawaii's Japanese community, portraits were idealized statements of an individual, a couple or family. It was not for themselves, but for their family members and relatives and friends back in Japan. The message is clear: We have attained material success; we made the right decision to leave Japan.

In one poignant Teragawachi portrait, a muscular man in the costume of a *sumo* wrestler stands with his legs apart in a stolid stance, hair slicked back, arms stiffly held out to his sides. Alongside, a boy imitates his father like a tiny mirror image. It's a universal statement of fatherly expectation and a son's earnest emulation.

In a Roaring Twenties image, five urbane and obviously middle-class women, all wearing hats and three wearing spectacles, exude a studied intellectual air. The woman in the center has a long neck like a figure in a Modigliani painting. What did these women do on afternoons? Meet for coffee and discuss a Paris Dadaist exhibition? Perhaps they read aloud to each other Fitzgerald's *The Great Gatsby*.

The more than 4,000 long-lost Teragawachi portraits are like letters in bottles thrown into the sea, suddenly re-surfacing half a century later. But unlike a letter, filled with words, a photograph's meaning is more elusive. There is no dictionary that can define the erotic curve of an upturned hand, or a child's half-smile. Usaku Teragawachi's photographic legacy illuminates a fascinating middle period in the history of Japanese in Hawaii — a time when they were still very much Japanese yet experiencing accelerating change.

— Ray Tsuchiyama

50

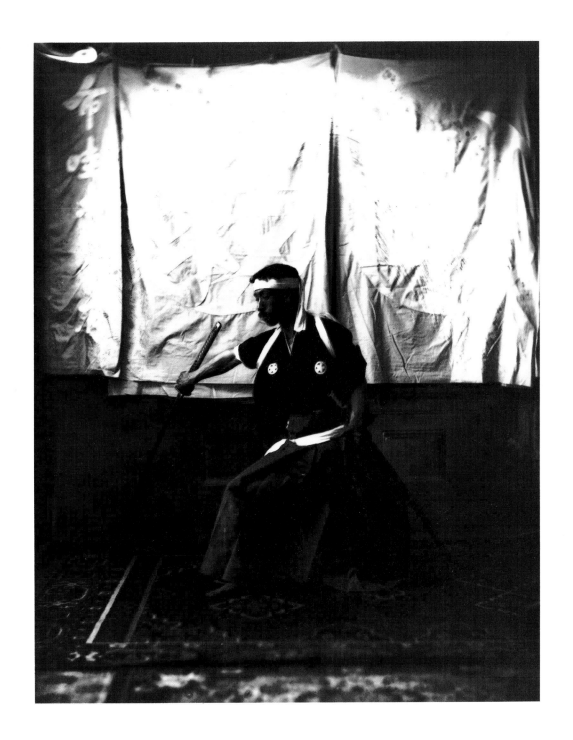

WORLD WAR II

When December 7, 1941 dawned in Hawaii, there were 160,000 persons of Japanese descent living in Hawaii—almost 40 percent of the Territory's population. Less than one-fourth of them were *issei,* or first-generation immigrants from Japan. The rest were Americans by birth. For all of them, Japan's attack on Pearl Harbor that Sunday morning not only shattered forever the Hawaii they knew, unleashing a war like the world has never seen, but it also made each of the 160,000 suspect to those who, out of racial prejudice or ignorance, saw no difference between them and the enemy who had unleashed the bombs on Pearl Harbor and Hickam Field.

Immediately following the Pearl Harbor attack, rumors raged through the Islands: people heard that a downed Japanese flier wore a McKinley High School ring; that Japanese sugar workers had cut arrows in cane fields pointing the way to Pearl Harbor; and that Japanese motorists blocked key roads with their cars during the attack. Immediately, or so it seemed, there were calls for evacuating all Japanese here to the Mainland, or at least to Lanai, never minding the fact that more than three-fourths of them were Americans by birth. Fortunately, their large numbers, and the urgency of building up military might in Hawaii, spared Hawaii's Japanese from the mass relocation and imprisonment that their mainland counterparts suffered. However, 1,441 Japanese in Hawaii—most but not all of them *issei*—were arrested and two thirds of them were imprisoned.

The Territory's military government ordered Japanese families to turn in their radios and weapons, special curfews were imposed, and gatherings were prohibited for Japanese in Hawaii. Suspicion and mistrust surfaced in everything from schoolyard taunts to the discharge of AJA members of the Hawaii Territorial Guard. "Until Pearl Harbor, I didn't think I was Japanese," many a *nisei* recalls.

Vindication—if there was any need for it—came in myriad ways. Just like good Americans everywhere, persons of Japanese ancestry in Hawaii pitched in with the war effort, buying war bonds,

Japan's attack on Pearl Harbor (left) devastated the American fleet. Preceding pages: Iuemon Kiyama hugs his son, Howard, on August 9th, 1946, at welcome home ceremonies held on the grounds of Iolani Palace, and some 3,000 Hawaii volunteers who created the 442nd Regimental Combat Team pose for a farewell portrait.

collecting scrap metal, donating blood and making slippers for wounded troops. "There was not one single act of sabotage committed against the war effort in the Hawaiian Islands during the course of the entire war," the FBI agent in charge of the Honolulu office said after it was over. "Nor was there any fifth-column activity in existence or evidenced here." That was indeed commendable, but the final proof of loyalty was provided by the 24,000 Americans of Japanese ancestry who served with the 100th Battalion and 442nd Regimental Combat Team in Europe and in the Military Intelligence Service in the Pacific.

The 100th Battalion, 1,300 Hawaii AJAs who were in the Army or National Guard when the war began, came first, spearheading the Allied push to Rome in 1943-44. Later, some 4,000 Hawaii and Mainland AJAs (Americans of Japanese Ancestry) of the 442nd Regimental Combat team joined the 100th in Italy in June of 1944. Together, they went on to compile an unsurpassed record of combat valor.

The 442nd did most of its fighting in Italy, but it is perhaps best known for a series of battles that raged in eastern France during the autumn of 1944. After three weeks of heavy fighting, the 442nd broke open a front that had been stalemated for months, liberated the key town of Bruyeres, rescued 211 trapped Texans of World War II's so-called "Lost Battalion" and suffered appalling casualties. For their valor, the men of the 100th and 442nd earned seven presidential unit citations, 18,143 individual citations, 9,486 Purple Hearts for casualties and the respect of America. When President Harry S. Truman welcomed them home from the war, he said: "You fought for the free nations of the world. You fought not only the enemy, but you fought prejudice—and you won." War correspondent Bill Mauldin put it a different way: "As far as the Army in Italy was concerned, the *nisei* could do no wrong. We were proud to be wearing the same uniform," he said.

Unlike the *nisei* soldiers fighting in Europe, those who fought in the Pacific were one of the best kept secrets of World War II. These 6,000 men of the Military Intelligence Service were credited with saving countless lives and shortening the war by two years. They fought in the land of their ancestors by gleaning priceless information about the enemy from captured documents and communications, and by convincing Japanese troops to lay down their arms and surrender.

After the war, General Joseph W. Stilwell, U.S. commander in the China-Burma-India Theater of Operations, summed things up this way: "The *nisei* bought an awful big hunk of America with their blood. We cannot let a single injury be done to them without defeating the purposes for which they fought."

—Mark Matsunaga

Home from the war: Ten Maui soldiers of the 100th Infantry Battalion relax on Oahu after their return from 18 months of combat in Italy. They are, standing, left to right, Pvt. Kenji Nikaido and Pvt. Nobuyoshi Furukawa; seated on the jeep's hood, Pvt. Edward Nashiwa, Pvt. James Kalei Kaholokula and PFC Richard Iriguchi; and standing about, PFC Hisao Tsutsumi, PFC Donald Uchimura, Pvt. Clifford Saruwatari, PFC Toshio Umetsu and Tech. Sgt. Hideo Sato.

Going For Broke

For thousands of Americans of Japanese ancestry in Hawaii, World War II meant combat . . .

One night in October of 1944, a young GI replacement joined section leader Turk Tokita's machine gun section —of H Company, 442nd Regimental Combat Team —in the woods outside Bruyeres, France. Tokita told the new soldier to dig in for the night.

The next morning, the 442nd attacked the Nazi-held town of Bruyeres.

"The sun was just coming up. It was a little dark, and when we hit the line, we just took it for granted he was following. In the thick of battle, we didn't stop to count heads. . . ."

Tokita was wounded by shrapnel two or three days later. The wound didn't heal until four years after the war, but Tokita didn't get to stay in the hospital very long.

Two weeks after he was wounded, in a hilltop forest a few miles closer to Germany than Bruyeres, the 442nd rescued the "Lost Battalion." It took a week. The men of the 442nd fought hole to hole and tree to tree until a bayonet charge finally broke through a ring of German soldiers surrounding Texans of the 141st Infantry.

That victory was sweet indeed, but war raged on —and so did the Four-Four-Two.

"They were so short of men, they pulled us out of the hospital —anybody who could walk and pull a trigger, right back into the line. It was snowing, cold, miserable," recalls Tokita.

"When I came back from the hospital, they told me, 'Hey, Turk, you remember this guy, you know he died; you left him over there.' The graves registration guys found him.

"We left him back there. He was dead. Jeez, I don't know how he died. I didn't even know his name. I still don't know."

. . . But there was more to the war than just combat for the nisei.

Before the Pearl Harbor attack, Katsugo Miho's father, a former Japanese language school teacher, ran the Kahului Hotel on Maui. He was also a special aide to the Japanese Consul General and personally attended ceremonies commemorating the 2,600th anniversary of the Meiji Dynasty in Japan in 1940.

"But we knew, and it was always understood, that Japan was Japan and Hawaii was Hawaii," recalls Miho.

When his father was arrested on Dec. 7, 1941, he said, "It was expected," because "before the war the FBI came to our house. I remember getting mad like hell. They didn't take off their shoes," said Miho.

When he volunteered for the 442nd Regimental Combat Team in 1943, he talked it over with his brother Katsuaki.

"He had already been accepted to go to Tulane Medical School, so I told him, 'You stay out, I'll volunteer for the family.' But he said, 'This is different.' Each individual had to do what he thought was right.

"He would have been of greater service to us nisei and Hawaii if he completed his doctor's training. There weren't too many Japanese doctors in Hawaii then."

But Katsuaki disregarded Katsugo's advice and also volunteered for the 442nd.

After he had died in a truck accident

The 442nd color guard, above, salutes during a French Armistice Day ceremony held on Nov. 11, 1944. At right, the 100th Battalion marches through bombed out Livorno, Italy, on its way to receiving its first presidential unit citation.

60

in Alabama, Miho took his brother's ashes to his father, who was then imprisoned in a relocation center at Missoula, Montana.

Miho received a cool reception. "They couldn't understand what was going on, because I had an urn with an American flag."

. . . The war finally ended, but certain personal "battles" lingered . . .

Shortly after Japan surrendered in August of 1945, Bob Tsuda went looking for his uncle — his father's brother — in Hiroshima. Tsuda was then a jeep driver attached to U.S. Army intelligence.

The Hiroshima railroad station "was jammed with people," Tsuda recalls. "It was one of the few buildings standing.

Everybody kind of turned and looked at me. I felt kind of lousy, but they were more scared than anything else.

"I was in an American uniform, and I still had my firearms with me, so I took them off.

"I didn't see any other GIs around, but could have been. I was so concerned about my uncle." Tsuda began searching for his uncle, but soon discovered that "I didn't know where to go because the whole city was flattened." In the end, says Tsuda, "I never found him.

"Later on, I found out he died in The Bomb. I think the whole family got wiped out."

It was about that time that Daniel K. Inouye went into a barbershop in California to get a haircut.

An army captain from Honolulu, In-

ouye wore the Distinguished Service Cross, the nation's second-highest award for valor, on his uniform. His right sleeve was empty. He had lost his arm and earned the medal by courageously attacking a German machine gun position in Italy.

The barber refused to cut his hair, however, because he was a "Jap."

During October of 1984, nearly four decades after World War II, a small group of *nisei* veterans revisited the former Nazi concentration camp at Dachau that they had helped liberate. A Japanese network television crew showed up to film the ceremonies. Muttered one *nisei* veteran: "They better make sure they say we're from Hawaii, not Japan Japanese."

— Mark Matsunaga

GOVERNOR ARIYO

CORKY '85

POSTWAR BOOMS

The Japanese-American soldiers of the 100th Battalion, the 442nd Regimental Combat Team and the Military Interpreters had departed Hawaii under a cloud of suspicion. They returned to the Islands as certified American heroes. Throughout the war they'd made great press: They were military units made up of Japanese-Americans and they courageously fought the Axis powers of Germany, Italy and Japan. They'd been heavily decorated, and a nation had celebrated their right to be called not "Japs," but Japanese-Americans, or better, simply Americans.

Despite their successes, however, Hawaii's returning veterans knew that their victory was incomplete. The society to which they returned remained stratified. Hawaii's dominant *haole* elite enjoyed excessive economic, political and social power throughout the Islands. With such hometown realities in mind, the Japanese-American veterans set about making their lives.

Fortunately, these men were aided by that most enlightened legislation of the postwar era, the GI Bill of Rights. "The GI Bill was the key," says Mike Tokunaga, a 100th Battalion veteran and now the Deputy Director of the State Department of Accounting and General Services. "Without it I'd be working on the Pioneer Plantation in Lahaina today." The GI Bill offered Tokunaga and others a chance to receive the education which their parents had so long valued but which plantation wages often proved insufficient to finance.

They returned to the Manoa campus of the University of Hawaii or to universities on the mainland. They lived on their $75 per month stipends, resided in quonset hut veterans' dorms, and they drank and gambled with their war-time buddies much as they had half-a-world away in the trenches of Europe.

After graduation the influence of Japanese-American veterans began to be felt in the community. They were a potent force: Seventeen thousand veterans, well-educated by the GI Bill, representatives

George Ariyoshi, who became governor of Hawaii, shakes hands with his mentor, Governor John Burns, in 1973, two decades after Burns formed the Democratic Party coalition that eventually defeated Hawaii's long powerful Republicans and gave Japanese and others a voice in Island politics. Preceding pages: Newspaper cartoonist Corky Trinidad's very graphical view of postwar Japanese Hawaii.

of Hawaii's largest single ethnic group, and determined to find a place for themselves in Island life.

Many turned to politics. An ex-cop named John A. Burns, who had defended the loyalty of Japanese-Americans during the war, recruited veterans into the heretofore powerless Democratic Party. The young *nisei* made natural recruits. Their clubs, the 442nd and the 100th, provided ready-made organizations for political use. Their youth and energy promised long-term commitment to the cause. Their education provided leadership skills unknown among any other ethnic group save the dominant, and smaller, *haole*. And they were motivated. "We were convinced that we deserved something better than the plantation and second-class citizenship," Dan Inouye remembered. "We wanted to exert ourselves and participate in developing Hawaii and in making policy. Those were exciting, almost intoxicating ideas."

In the elections of 1954, Inouye and his war-time comrades got their chance. The Democratic Party forged a coalition of Japanese-Americans and organized labor to seize control of the Territorial Legislature. Throughout the remainder of the decade and the 1960s, Japanese-Americans held legislative seats proportionately higher than their presence in the general population.

Following Hawaii's admission as a state in 1959, the United States House of Representatives welcomed its first member of Japanese ancestry, island Democrat Daniel K. Inouye. Three years later Inouye won a seat in the United States Senate. In the 1962 election, John Burns became Governor. He used his patronage to open government offices to Hawaii's own, including many Japanese-Americans. In the same election, 100th Battalion veteran Spark Matsunaga won election to Congress. Two years later a Japanese-American lawyer named Patsy Takemoto Mink joined Matsunaga in the U.S. House.

Politically, the decade of the 1960s belongs to Hawaii's Japanese-Americans. In the state Legislature, men named Nadao Yoshinaga, Nelson Doi, Sakae Takahashi, John Ushijima and Tony Kunimura reacted against their plantation pasts by enacting some of the most progressive labor legislation in the nation. They committed themselves and the state to educational opportunity for all by allocating a large proportion of state revenues to the public school system and the University of Hawaii.

Politics provided patronage for the Japanese-Americans involved. Those who chose business, however, found their ambitions more difficult to realize. Says Masaru "Pundy" Yokouchi, a Maui real estate developer: "We're not very entrepreneurial. We tend to put our heads down, *samurai*-style, and bull ahead." And in the immediate post-war years, the largest enterprises in the state still discriminated against non-Caucasians. In 1949 a young veteran with a degree in labor relations received only one return call from the five major companies to which he applied. That came from Mits Fukuda, a personnel officer at Castle and Cooke, who would rise to a vice-presidency in that *kamaaina* firm.

Hawaii's Japanese-American businessmen did it on their own. Sgt. Herman Teruya died at the battle of Monte Cassino, but his brother and fellow 100th Battalion member, Wallace, brought home

World War II produced many successful veterans, including U.S. Senator Spark Matsunaga, who was wounded twice in Italy with the 100th Infantry Battalion, and (preceding page) U.S. Senator Daniel K. Inouye, who lost his right arm after he courageously attacked a German machine gun nest in Italy.

Herman's dream of opening a modern supermarket. On April 29, 1949, Wallace and Alvin Teruya and their cousin Kami Uyehara opened their first Times Supermarket in McCully. By 1985 Times was in 15 Oahu outlets and is now the second largest supermarket chain in the Islands. Not far behind was the Star Market chain, owned by the Fujieki brothers.

At the onset of World War II, Hawaii's military governor closed all Japanese-owned banks. In the early 1950s, a group of Japanese-Americans founded Central Pacific Bank. A few years later a second *hui* led by James Morita established City Bank. Japanese-Americans moved into the savings and loan field as well; Masayuki Tokioka and his sons, Lionel and Franklin, made International Savings the ceterpiece of several family-owned institutions.

In 1919 Peter Fukunaga opened a small automobile repair shop in Haleiwa. Subsequently he obtained the Chevrolet automobile agency in Wahiawa and Waipahu. By 1985 his son, veteran George Fukunaga, had built his father's firm into a diversified retailing company called Servco Pacific, the thirteenth largest business in Hawaii.

And so the story went, in retailing, real estate, finance and a host of other businesses.

Hawaii's Japanese-Americans entered the professions in impressive numbers as well. Throughout the post-war period, for example, they have dominated the teaching profession. Governor William Quinn appointed Wilfred Tsukiyama the first Japanese-American Chief Justice of the Hawaii State Supreme Court. Masaji Marumoto, Jack Mizuha, Bert Koybayashi, Kazuhisa Abe, Edward Nakamura, Yoshimi Hayashi and James Wakatsuki would also rise to the Supreme Court. In 1974 MIT-trained engineer Fujio Matsuda began a decade long tenure as the President of the University of Hawaii. In medicine, heart specialist Richard Mamiya gained national renown for his work. And in 1985 Ellison Onizuka, a Kona-born major in the United States Air Force, orbited the earth as an American astronaut.

By the mid-eighties, Japanese-American political power in Hawaii had waned. Demographics worked against them. In 1954 Japanese-Americans constituted 37 percent of the Islands' resident population; in 1980 they made up 25 percent. *Nisei* no longer dominated the state legislature, and in 1985 Governor Ariyoshi was in the midst of his final term in office. Only Kauai Mayor Tony Kunimura and U.S. Senators Dan Inouye and Spark Matsunaga remained of the generation of veterans who had struggled to claim a place for Japanese-Americans in Hawaii's political life.

But their victory was secure. As an ethnic group Japanese Americans enjoyed the third highest personal income level in the State, the highest of any ethnic group which constituted over 10 percent of the population. Their children were prospering, and they could build their futures confident that their parents and grandparents had provided them with solid foundations.

—Dan Boylan

January 24, 1985. In Space: Ellison Onizuka was *floating*. But he wasn't surprised. Just a few hours ago, he sat perched atop a giant Roman candle that lit, roared him loose of gravity and everything else he'd known, and became part of a switch-lined, two-ton bubble orbiting the Earth at a dizzying rate.

Each switch or button lining the cabin served a different function: some kept the steel bubble from exploding; some materialized food and drink; a critical few deployed a McDonnell Douglas-powered "spy" satellite at some targeted point in space.

"You must be able to handle any of 6,000 malfunctions—2,000 of which may force you to abort . . ." clicked Ellison's brain. NASA's training drills were thorough.

But the Air Force major's mind wasn't on exploding. As he peered outside the window, land and ocean masses zoomed by. ("There goes Africa . . .") Blues and browns converged in blackness and, rimmed by rosy sunrise, the turning globe struck him as fragile.

North America edged out of view; a tiny string of islands—Hawaii?—dotted the Pacific; and when Australia filled the window, Onizuka pulled away.

Weightless or not, it was time to get back to work.

Though America's first military shuttle flight took a low profile, the media hailed Hawaii-born Ellison Shoji Onizuka as the world's first astronaut of Asian ancestry. It also publicized the fact that he had lifted macadamia nuts, Kona coffee and pineapple to new heights (literally).

After he got back, though, the newly-promoted lieutenant colonel didn't wax poetic about his journey's sights or significance. The three days aloft were "just another trip," he said. And he "looked forward to the next one" this November. Reporters sighed—but expected as much. For, unlike the seven Mercury pioneers of President Kennedy's New Frontier, the new astronauts were about as flamboyant as Wonder bread. In fact, they often proved to be the most reluctant heroes of all.

At 38, Onizuka doesn't look like a national hero; he looks more like a tax attorney or accountant. Or an engineer—which he is. His hair's short, his demeanor placid. His gaze is direct, but not bold. Onizuka talks low and smiles often, but he rarely laughs aloud. In short, he's the kind of man who looks at-home in a suit and tie.

But a space suit? Onizuka chuckles. Credibility was always a problem, and a big reason why he kept his dream quiet while growing up in Keopu, a tiny, unheard-of corner of north Kona.

"How do you convince people you want to go to the moon?" he asks. "Do you say, 'Hey, I want to be an astronaut and work in the space program, be part of the next interplanetary space effort out on Mars?' I mean, people would think you're missing a few screws. They were still using kerosene stoves back then. We didn't have TV either, but we never missed it," he says. "We had other things to do." Like swimming at the beach, exploring caves, hiking as a boy scout—or even picking coffee.

Born of immigrant sugar workers from Japan, Ellison's parents, Masamitsu and Mitsue, owned a small farm and a mom-'n-pop store along Mamalahoa Highway, which isn't a highway at all, but a narrow road that winds through a hillside. They instilled in their four children Old World values which any first two generations settling into America deemed sacred—namely, hard work, perseverance and loyalty to the community. Foremost in that ethic was getting a good education. "My folks," he recalls today, "like all my friends' parents, always stressed that 'As long as you've got that, you have a real tool to better yourself with.' Very few families that came here to work could pass on much more than a chance at education. But I guess the feeling was once you had that, no one could take it away from you."

So Elli excelled. He played varsity sports at Konawaena High School, wrote for the school paper, and served as treasurer for his class, the state-wide student organization and the Young Buddhists' Association. He also remained active with Boy Scout activities, and even headed the statewide 4-H Federation—an organization which prepares rural youngsters for careers in agriculture and livestock.

Like many of his classmates, he'd briefly considered being a coffee farmer, but his father encouraged him to stick with his studies.

So in '64, Onizuka enrolled at the University of Colorado as an aerospace engineering major. He was assisted by an ROTC scholarship, and, at a time when other students were burning flags and draft cards, Elli felt a dogged sense of patriotism. "These days, things are a little different," he says. "But when I was growing up in Hawaii, kids were proud to wear their uniforms to school. I guess I just stayed that way."

March 9, 6:40 p.m. In the belly of a United Airlines carrier circling low over the Pacific, Onizuka sits back, in a rare moment of privacy.

Ever since 1978, when he began training up to 90 hours a week in Houston, his life was a big blurred schedule. His wife, Lorna, recalls that her own "greatest hurdle" was adjusting to his work demands and "being mom and dad" to Janelle, 15, and Darien Lei, 9.

He was just three years older than Darien when he'd confided his dream to one special person. "I wanna go into space when I grow up," he told his grandfather. Not knowing what "space" meant, or who John Glenn was—but just what calloused hands did—the old man urged flatly: "Do something *useful*."

Those grandfatherly words echoed over the years. In 1982, when Ellison represented the U.S. at a shuttle exhibit in Japan, he afterward visited the Onizuka ancestral tomb in Fukuoka, where he prayed for his family.

The click of seat belts remind him: in ten minutes, we'll be there. Anticipation at seeing familiar faces rises up—but without illusion. No lazing at the beach, he thinks. Instead, interviews, speeches and glad-handing await him in Kona. But no one said being a hero was easy. Least of all, during these hometown visits sentimentally described by NASA as "routine post-flights."

Suddenly, below, in the dusk, an island looms. It was just a dot when seen from the *Discovery*, but it's sprawling now. Ellison smiles . . . ready . . . because in a way, coming back with good news had been an integral part of the mission from the start.

The Kona Surf Hotel lanai is a riot of good will, *muumuus* and pidgintinged voices. Carnation and plumeria smells fill the air. A huge banner—"Welcome Home, Ellison! Konawaena High, Class of '64"—hangs high over all. Restless eyes scan the walkway where *he's* supposed to appear. Heads bob to check wrists: 8:10 p.m. A camera-laden man tells his notepad-toting partner that he saw the police-escorted limo pull up 45 minutes ago . . .

Bill Knutson, president of the local Chamber of Commerce, nods to Mitsue Onizuka on the walkway: "Now we know how he felt when his flights were delayed, yeh? He got used to it . . . and it's our first time. But why complain? We still have 1,000 who came here tonight to see him."

Nearby, Ellison's former Explorer Scout troopmaster, Norman Sakata, tells a reporter softly, "This is a proud moment." Sakata's wife says that Norman was "in high heaven" the day Ellison blasted off the launch pad. "Norman was getting in the shower when we saw the rocket on the news. So we called, 'Daddy, hurry—Ellison's going up!'" She laughs, "—so he wraps a towel around, runs out and starts cheering at the TV: 'Yaay, Elli!'"

Sakata recalls a letter Onizuka wrote to him in 1982 from Houston, thanking him for his guidance: "It's only because of [family and friends] that people like me can grow up in the coffee fields of Kona and fly on the Space Shuttle . . . As Alan Shepard once said, 'It's easy to reach out and touch the moon when you're standing on the shoulders of giants'—and you are all giants.'"

Suddenly, a knot of bodies surges onto the clogged walkway. Loud voices prompt TV cameras to glare on one face in the middle. *His*. Ellison's smiling. Fronted by his wife, daughters and bodyguards, he's bashful in a dark suit. He blinks at the artificial sun. Hard to focus on the faces . . .

The governor's wife, Jean Ariyoshi, is among the first to grab his hand: welcome back. Then, in one fluid motion, relatives pour *maile* and kisses over him.

Mitsue hesitates on the side. Is it my turn? I don't want to get in the way. Wait, someone calls out—"Let Mitsue go through!" The bodies part; the short, birdlike woman wearing thick glasses inches forward. And with an orchid *lei*, she claims her son in front of everybody. His long embrace claims her back.

Then the tidal crowd pushes both toward the dining room. It's "Ellison Onizuka Day!" A day for glory and speeches and hometown pride.

—Naomi Sodetani

71

Jesse: 'More Japanese Than Japanese'

Jesse James Kuhaulua (also known as Takamiyama, Daigoro Watanabe, and, now, Azumaseki Oyakata) is a luminary in the true sense of the word: he lights up every room he enters, and he brightens the lives of everyone he encounters. For twenty years—from 1964 to 1984—Jesse's intensity and dedication illuminated the *sumo* ring. Now he has retired, and although there is no doubt that he will be a great coach and a visionary recruiter of *sumo* talent, there is still a sense that a light has gone out in the *sumo* arena. Jesse's torch of accomplishment, popularity and—yes—heroism cannot simply be passed on to the next foreign-born *sumotori* in line: there will never be a "second Jesse," for he is totally unique, both as a person and as a historical phenomenon. He has often been described as "one in a million," but the fact is that even the seemingly farfetched "one in a novemdecillion" would probably be an understatement.

Jesse has often been accorded the ultimate compliment by his Japanese admirers: "He's more Japanese than the Japanese," they say. What they mean by this enigmatic-sounding statement is that he has developed a perfect sense of the Japanese proprieties and social rituals, and an uncanny sensitivity to his own unusual and unprecedented place in Japanese society. No matter what the occasion or the setting, Jesse is unfailingly modest, courteous, cheerful, charming and generous with his time, and he somehow manages to maintain a dignified demeanor without sacrificing his natural spontaneity and charm. If the situation is a relaxed, informal one, the slapstick-comical side of Jesse's nature sometimes surfaces, and he will clown

around a bit, mugging photogenically (to the delight of the ubiquitous photographers, who know a God-sent subject when they see one), and telling jokes in his trademark voice. (If a slightly hoarse voice is described as a "frog in the throat," then Jesse would seem to have swallowed the entire pond. In fact, the idiosyncratic huskiness of his voice is due to an accidental injury to his vocal chords, which occurred during training. The condition is operable, and Jesse has said that he might consider having the operation after his retirement.)

Jesse's popularity and visibility in Japan do not derive entirely from the *sumo* connection. He has also made a number of television commercials, the best of which are both artistic and hilarious. Perhaps the most highly acclaimed of these is one in which Jesse, dressed in a snazzy three-piece pinstriped suit which was probably not purchased off the rack, does a little soft shoe shuffle with all the grace and lightness of a 125-pound adagio dancer.

Jesse's charismatic presence, though, is just the tip of the iceberg—or, to use a metaphor more appropriate to such a quintessentially warm and luminous being, the end of the candle. His fine character—the strength, the kindness, the humility, the dedication, the wholesome values, the charitable activities, the devotion to his family—adds a deeper sort of glow to his already incandescent personality. Now, this flood of superlatives may seem somewhat excessive, but hyperbole is what heroes are all about—and anyway, in Jesse's case the hyperbole happens to be true.

When Jesse's life is viewed with the omniscience of retrospect, the Heavy

Hand of Fate would seem to be much in evidence. However, as in any life, it is hard to say where serendipity leaves off and destiny begins. In any case, Jesse's story thus far, in its most simplified form, has been so widely told that by now it must certainly be a part of the collective consciousness of the people of Hawaii and Japan. Surely everyone has heard how Jesse grew up in the small community of Happy Valley, Maui; how both of his legs were broken when he was ten years old, and his high school football coach suggested that he join the local amateur *sumo* group in order to strengthen his legs; how photographs of the young Jesse-as-amateur-*sumotori* came to the attention of the famous stablemaster Takasago in Tokyo; and how, after meeting Jesse and observing his evident talent for *sumo*, Takasago Oyakata issued an invitation to join his stable and become a professional *sumotori*. Jesse accepted the invitation—and the challenge—and went off to Tokyo, where he endured the cold, the unfamiliar food, the rigorous discipline, the sleep deprivation, the homesickness and, at first, the language barrier. After paying his dues in the lower ranks of *sumo*, Jesse eventually rose to *sumo*'s third-highest rank, *sekiwake*, and, in July of 1972, he became the first foreigner ever to win a tournament championship.

Jesse has frequently been called an "Iron Man" because of his incredible durability in the physically and emotionally attritional sport of *sumo*. Many *sumotori* hang up their *mawashi* before the age of thirty, but Jesse continued to fight until a stubborn elbow injury forced him to retire within a month of his fortieth birthday. *Sumo*,

with its abrupt, twisting throws and apocalyptic collisions is very conducive to injuries, but Jesse somehow managed to climb into the ring (often held together at crucial junctures by multiple layers of Ace bandages) for 1,425 consecutive bouts, thus setting a record which is not likely to be broken for some time. In addition to numerous other records for sheer toughness and continuity, Jesse also won the Outstanding Performance Award a record six times, and won twelve "Gold Stars" for upset victories over assorted Grand Champions—the most in the history of *sumo*. Certainly there is a small irony in the fact that Takamiyama—the most internationally famous *sumotori* of all time, and one who has virtually rewritten the record books of the sport—has not one corpuscle of Japanese blood (although he is now a naturalized Japanese citizen) and more or less stumbled into the world of *sumo* by the most serendipitous—and-or fateful—of routes.

Epilogue: The human race has a well-known trait which might be called "historical myopia"—that is, the failure to recognize and appreciate its true heroes until after they are dead. In the case of Jesse James Kuhaulua/Takamiyama/Daigoro Watanabe/Azumaseki Oyakata, however, the collective vision both of the media and the masses appears, for once, to be 20/20. Everyone seems to be aware that there is a genuine hero among us, and that we are all involved in the making of a living legend—if not an epic myth. This transfusion of heroism and delight is Jesse's gift to us, and all that we can give to him in return is our continuing admiration and affection.

—Deborah Boehm Gushman

At the "Na Mele '83 Hawaii Song-writers Conference," noted oldtimer Uncle Sol Bright told the *kupuna* he wasn't worried that the young ones would forget their words and music. When he looked at a young man in their midst, he felt those traditions were safe.

Indeed, he was right, because the young man, Larry Lindsey Kimura, is an ardent wellspring of Hawaiian lore who takes his role very seriously.

Called the foremost native language poet-song composer of his generation, Kimura, 39, also teaches Hawaiian language at the University of Hawaii and over KCCN radio waves on Sunday night. His list of lyrical accomplishments is impressive. He has:

— Co-penned with Eddie Kamae one of the most popular local ballads of the past 30 years, "E Ku'u Morning Dew," recorded—at last count—by 24 different artists and groups;

—Contributed seven songs to the first two Sunday Manoa albums;

—Co-written with Peter Moon two songs on the tradition-breaking (and -setting) "Tropical Storm" LP of 1979, and authored-spoke the introduction to Peter's controversial version of "Kaulana Na Pua";

—Written (in 1980) the poem on Keith Haugen's album about the historic activist "trespassing" of Kaho'o-lawe; and also a *mele* celebrating the "Wa'a Hokule'a," the great sailing canoe that has symbolized a reclaiming of Hawaiian "roots" for so many;

—Written the lyrics for "E Pili Mai," a recording by the Peter Moon Band which won the 1983 Na Hoku Hanohano Award for "Haku Mele: Best Song Written in the Hawaiian Language";

—Walked away with 1983's coveted Sid Grayson Award citing outstanding contribution to Hawaiian music;

And, finally, the Hawaiian Music Foundation says that no fewer than 21 of Larry's songs have been recorded to date.

No doubt about it. Larry Kimura is every bit the Hawaiian Renaissance Man, and except for some gray mixed into his black hair, he looks more like one of his own students than a celebrity in his field.

This slightly-built scholar-artist talks in an easy local lilt about his work—which, simply put, is to keep Hawaiian culture alive. Yet, behind his softspeak lies all the punch and clarity of *message*. His songwriting, he says, is just an extension of one's love of the language—which "conveys our values, how we perceive the world.

"The identity of the Hawaiians," he says, "is tied to *aina,* our homelands. But if the slopes are covered with tract homes—all you have left is yourself as an individual. And a major connection to one's self has to be language. It's the last link, and must not be lost."

It's somehow curious to hear Kimura embrace his Hawaiianness so—especially since that's just part of his "local" being. He too often wonders, "why I got so involved in that and not the Japanese side of my heritage. I guess because of the nature of my work, the other side doesn't get to pop up so much."

But when he goes home to see his family, the two sides merge again.

At a time when mixed marriages were rare, his *nisei* father, Hisao Kimura, had wed Elizabeth Lindsey, who came from the well-known Hawaiian-English Lindsey ranching family. In the closeknit Parker Ranch community, Larry's "grandfather, father and even some Japanese today can speak pretty good Hawaiian—almost all the ranch hands do."

Larry and his four siblings grew up as cultural hybrids in Waimea's also prominent Japanese-Hawaiian cowboy clan. The unique Kimura dynasty has, in fact, produced some of the best Japanese cowboys in the world.

Since 1908 (when Larry's grandfather came to Waimea) almost all of the Kimura males—including Larry—were teethed on ranching duties; and many worked into supervisory positions in the Parker Ranch hierarchy.

At home, the songwriter's childhood was influenced by his grandmother's living with them: their home had an altar and *furo* (Japanese "hot tub"); he'd tag along when she went to Buddhist services; and the five *"hapa keiki"* wore *kimono* she sewed for them to wear to community *bon* dances. Larry loved her stories told in broken pidgin English.

His Hawaiian mother and grandmother "got along fine. Mom learned some Japanese, and Baban knew some Hawaiian; she'd cook the rice and mom would eat her *poi* with *hashi*!"

The youngster was also close to his *tutu,* a native speaker of Hawaiian—but all he knew of the language then was "names of songs, birds and flowers—and simple phrases." It wasn't till he attended the Kamehameha Schools in Honolulu that his deep respect for the Hawaiian language was instilled.

His *sensei* (teacher) there, Dorothy Kahananui (who wrote *Let's Speak Hawaiian,* the standard beginner's text), "treated the topic seriously, sincerely—at a time nobody cared. I said, 'That's terrific! I know what she's talking about!' It was self-discovery in a true sense."

In 1968, he shared a class at the University of Hawaii with another part-Hawaiian, Palani Vaughan. The result: five of his songs ended up on a local classic, "Meet Palani Vaughan and the Sunday Manoa." He wrote two more for Sunday Manoa's follow-up LP—though at the time he still saw his songwriting as "just a hobby."

After serving two years in the Army, Larry began teaching Hawaiian language at the University. "I just figured, 'Wow, there's such a wealth of stuff here, not just for me but for everybody else. How can I make the language available to others, too?'"

Since 1971, Kimura has provided answers—increasingly musical—to that question. He recalls how Eddie Kamae approached him 13 years ago, to think up lyrics for his new song. After a visit back home, he played back Kamae's taped melody "and thought of the morning dew in Waimea. The first verse came instantly"—and the rest is modern Hawaiian musical history.

"E Kuʻu Morning Dew," a modern Hawaiian "classic," has been recorded not only by the Sons of Hawaii, but by the Makaha Sons of Niihau, Melveen Leed, Emma Veary, the Brothers Cazimero, Ohta-san, Sonny Chillingsworth, George Helm, Loyal Garner and Genoa Keawe—to name a few.

Those who've sung to Larry's words since then make up a list far longer than that, and at the same time a growing public response to Hawaiian music itself has reflected a new and heightened awareness of the native heritage—truly a renaissance.

This fervor to reclaim a "too long-ignored past" was the heart of a *movement*—and Larry was in its vanguard.

He composed one *mele,* "E Na Hawaiʻi," for "those striving to be Hawaiian in spite of all the odds one faces in becoming one—even here in *Hawaiʻi nei.*" Among others, it was created especially for a Hawaiian language radio program, "Ka Leo Hawaii," a project of

the University Hawaiian language club (which Larry still serves as advisor).

"There's a saying in Hawaiian, 'Ua ulu ka hoi,' which plays on the word *hoi,* a delicate variety of wild yam which grows in our forests when conditions are right, and *hoi,* or *hoihoi*—a feeling of rewarding interest. For many years this *hoi* remained quiet; now it sprouts in regeneration: *ua ulu ka hoi.*" It is a poetical expression which emphasizes that "a new spirit is born within, inspiring us to compose with *aloha.*"

What has also grown out of Larry's desire to preserve the culture—and is sprouting shoots now—is a pre-school program that's taught 100 percent in Hawaiian. Just a few blocks away, Pūnana Leo o Honolulu (meaning the "Language Nest of Honolulu"), the second of three such learning models Kimura has helped organize in the last three years, will start classes next week. The other two are in Kauai and Hilo.

Psychologists agree that children absorb first-language skills in the early years, he says, "so this is a necessary step if the Hawaiian language is to remain a part of our daily lives. It can't just be recorded in books and tapes—it has to be *spoken.*" Ironically, he adds, even Hawaiians are among those who ask, "'Why not just stick to English? Why keep a dead language alive?' [And] I just gotta say, 'Because Hawaiian is our own, not somebody else's. Because it has the right to live and be used—like Japanese, Filipino and Chinese. It's just as rich. Hawaiian expresses the soul of this place—no less than the others.' And when you can claim all the languages—together, mixed—then you can say: 'This is *our* home.'"

—Naomi Sodetani

'LOCAL' VISIONS

The first artist of Hawaii to achieve international recognition was a son of Japanese immigrants. Isami Doi of Kalaheo, Kauai, became an artist at a time when he had no precedents, no real role models, in the Japanese community. Though Hawaii's *imin* came from a rich visual tradition, they had to concern themselves primarily with work and their most immediate daily needs. Many children Doi's age still left school in the 5th or 6th grade to help their families, and art instruction was unheard of unless you were able to go on to high school or even to the University. The Honolulu Academy of Arts did not yet exist, and its art education program and fine Asian collection, which would later motivate many local aspiring artists, did not open until 1927, a year after Doi came to national attention in New York at the age of 24.

Doi's work, with its intense spiritual core and individualistic blend of Eastern and Western imagery, took him to the capitals and museums of the world. It is no wonder that he was looked upon as a leader, or older brother, by the whole wave of younger *nisei* who activated Hawaii's art scene in the 1940s and '50s. Many of these artists were then returning to Hawaii from the Chicago Art Institute, Chouinard, the Art Students League and other mainland art schools, where their postwar education was usually subsidized by the GI Bill.

This small art community banded together in an all-for-one spirit, trying to exhibit work wherever they could. Artists' clubs like Hui Nani and the Metcalf Chateau came and went, but a cast of characters began to emerge: Doi, Satoru Abe, Bumpei Akaji, Tadashi Sato, Tetsuo Ochikubo, Jerry Okimoto, Keichi Kimura, Takeo Gima, Sunao Hironaka and Sueko Kimura, among others.

The closest thing to corporate support these artists had was the now defunct Kuhio Grill in Moiliili. Filled with artwork either purchased, bartered or commissioned, it was a place one could enjoy a cold beer and family style *pupus* surrounded by art. It remained a favorite haunt of artists and university students until it closed in the late 1970s.

ISAMI DOI (1903–1965)
Left: No. 1 from *The Wayward Muse,* woodblock engraving (H×W: 2⅝″ × 2¼″), 1952
Pgs. 76–77: No. 7 *Hana Wai* from *Random Vintage,* woodblock engraving
(H×W: 1⅛″ × 2⅛″), 1941.

The lack of exhibition space during the postwar years prompted some artists to establish galleries that would show the new works being produced. In 1954, Sunao Hironaka helped create what remains Waikiki's most visible "gallery"—the Zoo Fence. Takeo Gima, meanwhile, opened Gima's Art Gallery in 1944. After relocating three times on Kalakaua Avenue, Gima's eventually became part of the new Ala Moana Center in 1959, and, until it closed in 1983, was a quiet, family-run oasis of Island art amidst Ala Moana's shopping throngs.

During the postwar period an increasing number of young artists ventured away from Hawaii to study and teach, to work in different environments. Many of these artists, among them Toshiko Takaezu, Ray Yoshida and Alice Kagawa Parrott, eventually settled on the mainland. Frequently their work would reflect their new surroundings and they would become aligned with the visual language of that region: Yoshida's intensely detailed and patterned paintings, for example, are a vital part of Chicago's electrified urban imagery, and Parrott now bases her weaving on the colors and landscapes of the New Mexican Southwest.

The converse has also been true: over the years there has been a steady influx of artists from outside Hawaii—many of them Japanese Americans, many of them Japanese nationals—who have relocated themselves here and have become important and integral members of Hawaii's art community.

The years have also produced other changes. Hawaii has become more westernized and cosmopolitan than ever before, though it still retains its strong ethnic identities. Third and fourth generation Japanese are usually unable to speak the language of their grandparents and are increasingly unfamiliar with the old traditions, but it is this very lack of awareness that has triggered in many a desire to re-examine family roots. Much of this interest has been inspired by worldwide interests in things Japanese—arts, crafts, business practices and technology—and as a result, heritage is being added to re-integrate into the Hawaiian culture.

The question of heritage was a thread that ran through Doi's work. In a 1952 interview he recalls that as a young man he wanted to be recognized as an outstanding Oriental artist, but that he abandoned this notion as he grew older and more experienced. This was not a denial of his family's ethnic background, but an acceptance of all the experiences that make each person an individual. Eight years later he said that his art was "an attempt to be conscious of my own heritage, to discover more about myself and my growing understanding of life, and to avoid getting on the bandwagon. . . ."

—Mary Mitsuda

All artworks in this portfolio are from the collection of the Contemporary Arts Center of Hawaii, except for the four copper and bronze sculptures by Bumpei Akaji on page 99 which are from the collection of Keiji Kawakami.

SATORU ABE (1926–)
The Seed, welded metal (H×W×D : 34″ × 34″ × 23″), 1970.

TADASHI SATO (1923 –   )
Surf and Water Reflections, oil on canvas (H×W: 84″ × 60″), 1969 – 1970.

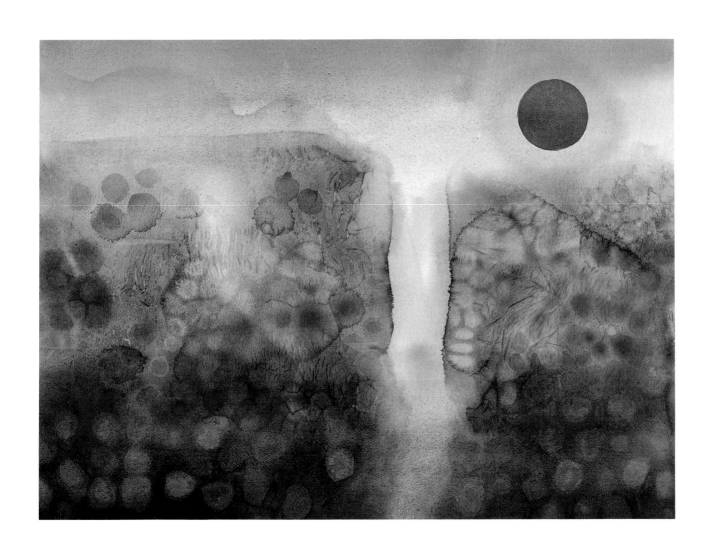

CHARLES HIGA (1933–)
Sea, Sun, Sky, watercolor on paper (H×W: 21″ × 28½″), 1969.

PAUL NAGANO (1938–)
New Planted Cane, watercolor on paper (H×W: 22″ × 29¾″), 1976.

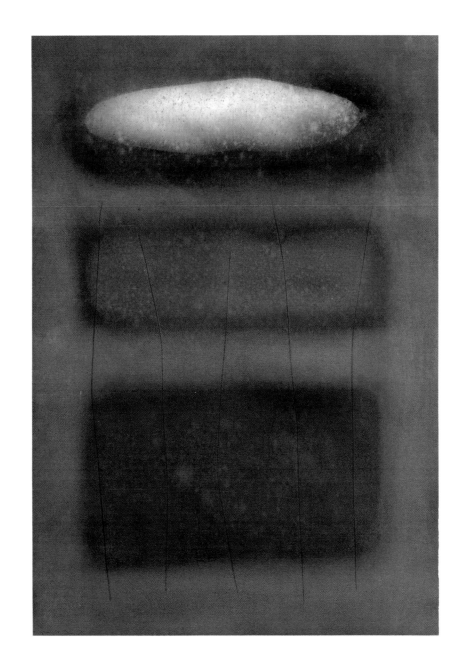

HIROKI MORINOUE (1947–)
Rock with Rectangular Forms, watercolor on paper (H×W: 30″ × 20″) 1979.

TETSUO OCHIKUBO (1923–1975)
Resonance, oil on canvas (H×W: 52″ × 72″), 1958.

86

MYLES TANAKA (1951 –)
Modern 5 Qualities: Women Series/No. 5, watercolor on paper (H×W: 22″ × 30″),
1978.

JOHN MORITA (1943–)
Great Grandmother Murashige's Funeral, photoetching
(H×W: 35½″ × 45½″), 1984.

WAYNE MUROMOTO (1954–)
Samurai Movie, lithograph (H×W: 13¾″ × 9⅞″), 1981.

BRIAN ISOBE (1954 –   )
Kabe Sequence (central panel of a tryptych), acrylic and watercolor on paper
(H×W: 30″ × 22″; entire tryptych, 30″ × 77½″), 1978.

SHIGE YAMADA (1933–)
Tea Bowls, oil on canvas (H×W: 20″ × 24″), 1981.

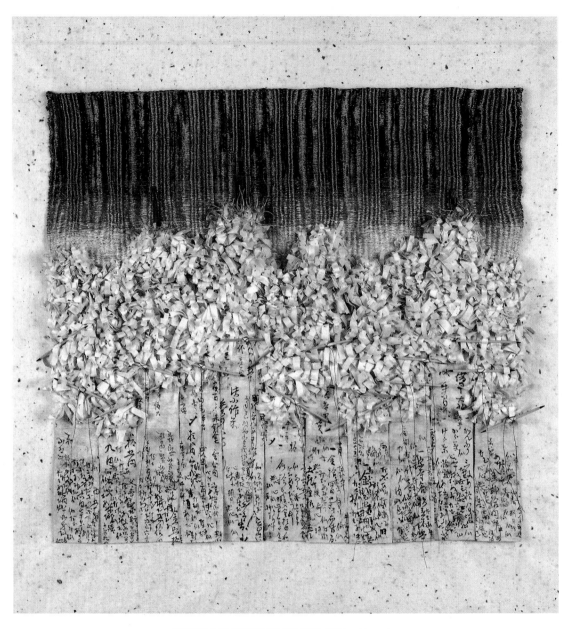

REIKO MOCHINAGA BRANDON (1933–)
Namuamidabutsu, copper, rice paper, cotton and bamboo
(H×W×D : 24″ × 23″ × 2″), 1984.

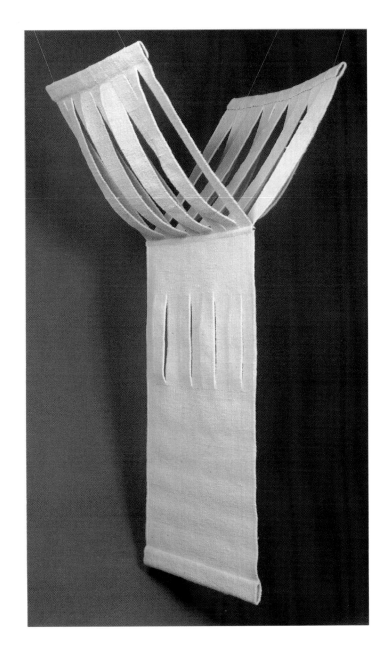

AKIKO KOTANI (1940 –)
Prince of Fundy, wool tapestry (H×W×D: 79″ × 37″ × 34½″), 1976.

RANDY HOKUSHIN (1951 –)
Linko, ceramic (H×W×D : 15″ × 21″ × 21″), 1977.

DAVID KURAOKA (1946–)
Da Union, Sandy Beach Kahalau, ceramic
(H×W×D: 11½″ × 17″ × 17″ ea. approx.), 1980.

NINA HAGIWARA PETERSON (1954 –   )
Tank Top, ceramic (H×W×D: 61″ × 22″ × 12″); *T-Shirt,* ceramic (H×W×D:
61″ × 22″ × 12″); and *Small Boy,* ceramic (H×W×D: 55½″ × 20″ × 12″), 1981.

MARIE KODAMA (1949–)
Frigidaire, clay and wire (H×W×D : 24″ × 18″ × 12½″), 1980.

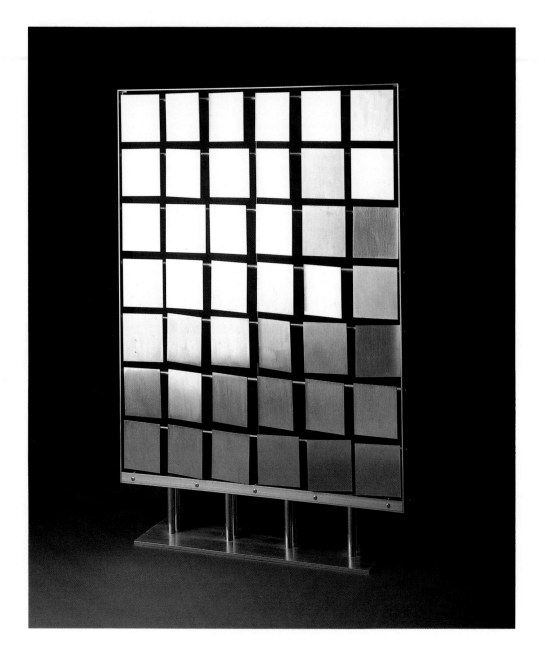

MAMORU SATO (1937 –   )
Scape 84-4, aluminum and steel (H×W×D : 42″ × 28″ × 8″) 1983.

BUMPEI AKAJI (1922–   )
From left to right: *Kokee Koa,* bronze (H×W: 11″ × 6″), 1962; *Difference of Opinion,*
copper and bronze (H×W: 15″ × 9¼″), 1980; *At Peace,* bronze (H×W: 11″ × 11″),
1964; *Man of the Year,* bronze (H×W: 26″ × 7″), 1978.

DOUGLAS DOI (1953–)
Parallel Realities Become a Substitute for Alchemy, polyester resin and wood
(H×W×D : 24″ × 66½″ × 12¼″), 1981.

Toshiko Takaezu: 'Madonna of the Clay'

Two years ago, on a curiously mild February day in Carlisle, Pennsylvania, a 62-year-old *nisei* woman potter stepped up to a podium and—amid a standing ovation—received the coveted Dickinson College Arts Award. This award, which has been presented only 11 other times in 25 years, was formerly received by artists such as the poet Robert Frost, the actress Dame Judith Anderson and a composer, John Cage.

The potter being thus honored was Hawaii's Toshiko Takaezu, the sixth child in a family of eight girls and three boys born to Shinsa and Kama Takaezu and raised in the plantation village of Pepeekeo on the Big Island and later on upcountry Maui farmlands.

The award cited Miss Takaezu for her excellence as an artist who combines her talent and ideas with discipline and an uncommon devotion to the pursuit of her art. She was commended for her aesthetic achievements over the past three decades—as a master potter, and for being a leader in the international revival of ceramic art in this century.

All that acclaim was pretty heady stuff for Miss Takaezu, who got into clay because she loved it, and who remains devoted to her art because it is her life and continues to challenge and fulfill her.

She said when she was informed about her award and realized what giants the former recipients were, "I got scared. Yes, scared. But I did use a better word when I mentioned that in my acceptance speech."

The thing she remembers about that speech is that "I was damn nervous."

However, and despite such nervousness, she channeled her considerable energy from "being-scared" to "doing-my-very-best" and within about six months she created a dazzling collection of more than a hundred new works—a colony of powerful, round moon pots, a "ceramic forest" of elongated cylindrical forms and a wide range of closed and open forms mixed with bronze pieces and related weavings—for an exhibition held at Dickinson's Trout Gallery in conjunction with her award.

That exhibition of her works—and their installation under her direction—was stunning. It moved the director of the gallery to state: "Like the performance of a great symphony, it could never be repeated with quite the same effect." That is, the exhibition itself was exciting and creative and had a life very much its own.

In a formal catalogue published to commemorate the occasion, the chairman of the college's Fine Arts Department defined Miss Takaezu's specialness in this way:

"Toshiko," he wrote, "exemplifies the type of artist for whom the challenge of aesthetic expression is not work but a way of life. As the artist herself has admitted, 'In my life, I see no difference between making pots, cooking and growing vegetables. They are all related. However, there is a *need* for me to work in clay. It is so gratifying, and I get so much joy from it, and it gives me many answers for my life."

The chairman said that Miss Takaezu's inability to distinguish between her artistic pursuits and herself as a person is "admirable" and noted that this same synthesis of art and life is reflected in her recounting of a visit to Japan in 1955 to study the tea ceremony to understand how to properly make tea bowls:

"I realized that even though I made bowls, I wasn't ready to make tea bowls. It was easy to make bowls, but to make tea bowls I had to be an individual. . . . It wasn't a question of technique; it was a question of being ready as a person."

The statement also reflects Miss Takaezu's basic understanding and reverence for the aesthetic and ethical tradition of Japan's culture of the tea, and provides an insight into the strong roots pottery has in Japanese, Chinese and Korean cultures.

Miss Takaezu's sense of oneness with clay is hence understandable, given her ethnic ties as well as her kinship with the earth through a farming heritage. Her love of gardening, and her pride in tending to a bountiful garden that grows everything from raspberries to onions, are quickly revealed. Her ceramic slide shows frequently include images such as a magnificent cabbage or a bunch of peaches, and she takes great pleasure in sharing her harvest with the constant flow of people who visit her home and studio.

In *The Penland School of Crafts: Book of Pottery*, Miss Takaezu spells out the intimate nature of her relationship with clay:

"One of the best things about clay is that I can be completely free and honest with it. And clay responds to me. The clay is alive and responsive to every touch and feeling. When I make it into form, it is alive, and even when it is dry, it is still breathing! I can feel the response in my hands, and I don't have to force the clay. The whole process is an interplay between the clay and myself, and often the clay has much to say.

When it is bisqued (first firing) it is no longer organic, but it comes alive again in the finishing touch of the last firing — in the interplay of glaze and form."

Her work is represented in numerous public and private collections and she has exhibited her work frequently in the last 20 years.

She began her studies at the Honolulu Academy of Arts and the University of Hawaii (under Claude Horan) and then studied at the Cranbrook Academy of Art in Bloomfield Hills, Michigan (under Maija Grotell).

She taught at Cranbrook and then at the University of Wisconsin and the Cleveland Institute of Art. She headed Cleveland's ceramics department before leaving for Princeton University in 1966, where she has been teaching since. Her studio and home are in Quakertown, New Jersey, but she travels to hold workshops and exhibits.

But wherever she is, each Tuesday she calls her 95-year-old mother, who lives in a peaceful valley in Honolulu, a few houses away in several directions from many of her other children. Miss Takaezu returns to be with her mother for several weeks each year. "She is truly a source of wisdom and I keep going home for the give and take," the artist said.

Miss Takaezu dedicated the Dickinson award to her mother because "it's her quiet encouragement, her efforts to help us understand integrity by example, that made it all possible."

In keeping with her family's way — and also in keeping with the Japanese way — she barely mentioned the Dickinson award to her family. And, aside from expressing happiness for her, no one made a big deal about it — even though it was.

The event did provide, however, an opportunity to focus sharply on the artist's journey over the last three decades in pursuit of her vision of purity and truth through her art. And rather than marking the end of her life's work, it served to celebrate the beginning of yet another stage of her work. She is, it appears, poised to soar.

Miss Takaezu says she once considered having a large family with lots of children and dogs and a large farm, "but I wasn't lucky in finding the right father for my children. Maybe I was afraid to find the right person. It takes the right combination to make it possible to have a family and to do your work as well. Maybe it was just not meant to be."

She said, "Life is a give and take. I know my weaknesses and I know my strengths. I have struggled to come to that. I'm still working. I'm still struggling."

So it is. Toshiko Takaezu, Hawaii's *nisei* madonna of the clay.

So it is. Toshiko Takaezu, an inspiration to a world starving for inspiration. Madonna of the clay. A very big deal. Indeed.

— Tomi Kaizawa Knaefler

The hushed sweetness of dawn is alive in this work by Toshiko Takaezu. Following pages: Takaezu inspects a scape of her spectacular moonpots.

103

Eiko Yorita was pau. *But instead of saying so, she pursed her lips, nodded twice, and shuffled to the far edge of the room. There she sat, her age-curled hands pressed into her lap. Her eyes searched for any last detail she might've missed; any flaw not smoothed under. But there was none.*

Six feet of molded fabric stood before her—red and gold brocade over layers of silks; stiff gilt cloth; and soft white gauze. Jutting toward the ceiling at odd angles were pearlescent and metal bangles; an ivory stick protruded from the middle.

And the thing moved.

Slowly, it slid across the mat; brocade scratched straw. Stopping a few feet away, before Yorita's full-length mirror, her "sculpture's" mouth dropped open. Reflected within was a perfect vision: a young woman dressed in full bridal ki-mono and headdress, with white skin and red lips, holding a sensu *(fan). Splendor itself, revisited from 12th Century Japan.*

But the same woman with shocked eyes was me. *In two and a half hours, Eiko Yorita had turned me into an utter stranger unto myself.*

Eiko, 86, is the local queen of *ki-mono*—and also among a mere handful of women who still practice the dying art of elaborate *kimono* dressing.

For some 46 years, she has readied *yome* for traditional weddings. And since 1953, Eiko has dressed Cherry Blossom Festival beauty pageant contestants in full regalia—helped in recent years by Lynn Mari Yorita (a granddaughter she trained). Appropriately, Eiko owns perhaps the largest *kimono* collection outside of Japan—more than 300 garments valued at $500 to $10,000 each—along with *obi*, accessories and wigs to match.

In her Kapahulu house, Eiko has filled a huge cabinet with miniature dolls from around the world. While growing up in Koochiken, on the island of Shikoku, she handcrafted dozens of these dolls, imagining that they were real.

Eiko came to Hawaii in 1919. Then in 1937, halfway through raising her family, she decided to become a beauty specialist. She tucked a suitcase under one arm, her youngest under the other, and returned to Japan. Makeup, hairdo and *kimono* dressing study usually took at least two years to complete. But not only did she train with Japan's best—the dresser of the Imperial Household—she studied hard and fast and returned to Hawaii with a diploma in a few months.

Eiko's business in Hawaii boomed—until Pearl Harbor also boomed and shut it down. Instantly, all ties to a Japan past were denied, buried or burned by *issei* and *nisei* who wanted to prove loyalty as *Americans*.

Eiko pulls pins out of her mouth— "Hard, pin up short hair." Our intimacy feels natural; she could be my grandmother.

"Put on juban now." She hands over a thin slip.

When I return to the mat, I find that she's arranged the hair ornaments, obi *and sashes, cords, purses and several ornate* kimono *in two rows. Suddenly, she slaps my legs. They* sprawled care-lessly. *"You no sit good, I scold you," she says. My* tabi'd *feet tuck back under, impeccably—as expected.*

Even after WWII, her business slumped. Many dressers quit the pro-fession, but Eiko kept on. When in 1953 the newly-formed Japanese Junior Chamber of Commerce began the Cherry Blossom Festival and beauty pageant, Eiko was asked to join the cause, and the charm and beauty lessons she had learned so well in Japan were applied to the young women in her charge. She would deftly fold and tie more than 30 individual garments (two to three *kimono* layers, three *obi*, *tabi*, etc.) onto each contestant.

Eiko became a celebrity. Her presence was sought at cultural events by politicians, businessmen—and even touring Japanese movie stars like Toshiro Mifune. A dusty framed photo shows Eiko in her heyday, posing with that handsome leading man. The picture says it all: In those post-war years, *kimono* dressing was reincarnated—as show biz.

The last time I wore a kimono, *I was 11 years old, readying for the Haleiwa* bon *dance with my cousins. Our mothers would tug off Mickey Mouse t-shirts and pull gangly arms into grace-ful sleeves that reached to knees. Hair was ouch'ed into chignons;* obi *became wings; some of us even got rouge on our cheeks.*

We loved all the fuss and drama that came with the "costume." When we finally flew out the door, giggling, our fathers, uncles and aunts cooed: "Kirei, ne! How pretty!" Magically, tomboys became girls. And, though none of us ever said it, we also felt curiously Japanese.

Now, I'm being groomed as a yome-san. *Behind me, Eiko winds a ten-foot long* obi *round my ribs, and my breath-ing is constricted. All I see are two hands passing it from right to left.*

Each time I try to see what she's doing,

Eiko scolds me to stay still. *Finally she mutters: "Wakaran . . ." Coming around me, she drapes* tsuno-kakushi *over my wig; it's meant to cover the horns of jealousy a new bride harbors toward her groom's lovers (past or future).*

She stares intently at the edge of the veil; her fingers coax it into evenness. Then Eiko works on my kimono *front— where it overlaps. When I try to straighten up (my neck is sore from bending) she says, irritated: "You listen. Don't move around! Don't make head up like this—" she mimics my chin-up, chest-out posture. "—Head look* ma-sugu *(straight ahead). Look down."*

Satisfied when I listen, *Eiko places silver slippers at my feet—then tucks a tiny silver purse halfway into my bodice. Since I heard that wives used to hide daggers in their clothes to commit sui-cide with their husbands (or avoid dis-grace), I ask her about this one.*

"No, this one no more knife," she says matter-of-factly.

Wakarimasen? Suddenly, it's clear —and she's right: I don't know how to be humble and obedient.

In 1983, the State Legislature read a resolution marking Eiko's official re-tirement after 30 years with the festi-val. She still does weddings, and has no intention of ever stopping—"I al-ways like this kind, see? That's why I do"—but demand for wearing the ki-mono has ebbed.

Part of the reason is because ki-mono rental is costly, time-consuming and you can't dance with guests. Even in Japan, where rental costs are higher, couples have begun opting for West-ern nuptials.

The revival of ethnic pride in the late Sixties to mid-Seventies boosted busi-ness a bit. "People see *Roots* on TV, so ring phone," Eiko recalls. The *sansei*, weaned in middle-class *American* com-fort, were eager to reclaim a Japanese heritage as part of their identity.

When Eiko said she'd dress me as part of my research ("You no under-stand, if other way . . ."), I was hon-ored—more than that, *intrigued*—by what her gift would yield; what of the past would I link with, embrace, reject? When I stood before Eiko, in her mir-ror I saw a "me" I did not recognize. I'd been draped in an exquisite layered body, but didn't know how to *move* in it; I held my sensu with proper deli-cacy, but had no modern *use* for it.

Eiko molded me with Zen-like atten-tion, into a living sculpture. But she couldn't curb my feelings of impa-tience, frustration—or *love of running*.

Nor could I.

So, the last bit of makeup is off, my t-shirt is back on, and I marvel at the cast-off layers lying on the mat like a heap of moultings: *Kimono*, orna-ments, wig—each trace of perfection that Eiko labored so long to achieve took seconds to destroy. Now, Eiko grabs my shoulders, smiling: "You *wakarimasu ka*? Understand now?"

She starts forming the garments into careful stacks—and I feel a jarring loss. Would *she* understand if I told her that, while in her *kimono*, my hands naturally felt like *folding*?

And that I felt like a queen, taking slow, small steps. And that I admire her spirit for showing me how sublime a vision can be—even if it lasts but an instant.

—Naomi Sodetani

If the Japanese in Japan are said to be masters of paradox, it can be argued that the Japanese in Hawaii bear a healthy dose of irony. Where that sense exists, it's strong. It reaches across centuries, continents, hemispheres and generations to blaze across a big screen in neon and bamboo: *Sansei*.

Abundant expressions of that irony can be found in the work of some of Hawaii's *sansei* artists, who are singing wordless praises to the ancient Japanese aesthetic while they carve their own firm niche in the fringe occupied by the *avant-garde*.

The Showman: In the late Seventies, when the highbrow Paris fashion world was all atwitter over the return of Japanese designer Kansai Yamamoto, a young man from Hawaii could be seen raiding the French department stores for some cotton knit underwear. Having just walked away from a Rockefeller fellowship to attend the Yamamoto showing, Amos Kotomori was resolute.

"I didn't have the clothes to wear, so I layered French underwear," he says. "They were long johns, knits and cottons of different textures. I cut some sleeves, showed off the trims, wore a *kimono* sleeve as a scarf, and rounded out the outfit with Levi's and funky shoes.

"There I was, in the midst of people dressed to kill, and my outfit cost 30 bucks at the most. Later on I took fabrics and pictures of my designs and knocked on Paris doors with my *furoshiki*."

The *furoshiki*, or Japanese gift-giving cloth, contained the forerunners of his later collections. In a few years Kotomori, now wearing his grandfather's

hakama, or traditional Japanese overskirt, went from knocking on doors to bowing to applauding audiences gathered alongside *haute couture* runways. Long before *sushi* became *au courant*, champagne and *sushi* flowed at his showings: There were hundreds of extravagant originals aglitter with sequins, beads, hand-painted silks and flowing *kimono* shapes. There were growing lists of clients, fashion tours to the mainland, and demands for stylings and weddings, each outshining the other. And then there was the 1985 Kanyaku Imin centennial fashion show, where metallic confetti rained upon Kotomori and his show-stealing collection of bridal gowns, wearable art and contemporary adaptations of plantation clothing.

Kotomori's penchant for mixing *kimono* shapes with glitzy metal, and for staging surrealistic fashion shows, strikes one as very *chic* indeed. But when he returns home from a big show and long bows before adoring fans, he walks into a living room imbued with the aesthetics of the East. "This is my grandmother's teapot," he points out. "And that's her bronze rice pot over there. I have my grandfather's things all over the place. Nothing in this house is new."

The Shaman: While the showman's path is a visible one, the shaman's is very private. Like a shaman, artist Morris Umeno seasons his creations with a reverence for ritual and symbol. He's also big on layers—layers of meaning and layers of waxed newspaper and bamboo that suggest wrapping, containment, and mystery.

Wrapping and unwrapping, says Umeno, is a ritual complete in itself. "There's the surface, but there's al-

ways something underneath, and always a little surprise. You could call my works ritual objects, but they're not necessarily religiously inclined. A shrine, for example, is also a container for an inner something."

Umeno's "Matsuri Festival" is a portable sculpture inspired by Shinto festivals in Japan, where people carry miniature shrines through the streets. "Wish pieces" of plastic, *origami* and glass beads dangle daintily beneath hundreds of batik strips hand-tied in traditional Japanese knots. "Whacko on the Loose," a hanging of bamboo, wire, electrical materials and bits of plastic and celluloid, is endearingly eccentric with a Japanese essence.

"Everything I do is inspired by Japanese culture," Umeno notes. "It's the result of growing up Japanese, rather than derived from the religion itself or studying a particular philosophy. It's not really conscious, like taking an oriental theme. It just happens to come through because I come from an oriental background.

"Someone told me once that when you do work, you have to fall back on your experiences. That's what I'm doing. You have to pull them out of something. Images don't come from nowhere."

For Umeno, growing up Japanese meant living in a Buddhist household with a Shinto shrine and all its accoutrement and rituals. It meant, he says, pounding *mochi*, washing his grandparents' gravestones, and carrying lanterns during the *o-bon* season.

"Even the presentation of food was different. The feeling was that the table is also a rectangle, and when you place the food on the table, you don't just put it down, you put it in its proper

Sansei designers include (from left) Kotomori, Kimura and Umeno.

place in the rectangle. It goes back to an awareness of nature and how everything is in harmony."

The Gatekeeper: Surrounded by Edwardian houses and Aubrey Beardsley's work, Ann Kimura was teaching in England and planning to move to Africa so her husband could head the chemistry department in a Tanzania college. One day, in a British museum, she stumbled upon a *katagami*, or Japanese stencil, exhibit.

"I said, 'What is this?'" Kimura recalls. "'This is Japanese. How come I don't know about it?' Gradually it dawned on me: I'm *Nihonjin*. How come my work isn't being influenced by my own culture?"

Temari, Hawaii's thriving center for Asian and Pacific fiber arts, was conceived with that realization. Years later, the school Kimura founded continues to make its mark on the lives of thousands of students and professionals as an open door for exchange, growth, and training. Many master craftsmen have come from Japan through Temari to conduct workshops here in Japanese dyeing, weaving and papermaking techniques. For those who enter its gates, tradition lives.

"The traditions were going to die," Kimura notes. "They were going to fade away and there was no way for our artists here — our people — to see our links to our past. As rebellious as our parents initially used to view us — as being kind of whacko, artists, crazy — I think they've accepted us and the way we express this acculturation. And I think we've done it. We've found a way to express ourselves without selling out, and without embarrassing our parents."

—Jocelyn Fujii

Blind Lilikoi, self portrait

NEW LIGHT WAVES

During every generation there emerges new images that depict the times. For each new generation since the turn of the century, photography has been a unique and most useful invention that has provided us with a clear visual document of the reality of the times. In the hundred years since the first Japanese immigrants arrived in Hawaii, countless numbers of photographs by Japanese-American photographers lay forgotten in vaults and in family photo albums. To celebrate this Centennial, this publication journeys through this photographic experience from the past to the present. Early camera works, in general, reflected a very formalistic view of the camera as a tool to merely record events and represent reality. The camera now acts less as a medium for information and more as a medium for expression. Photographic concerns deal more with private observations, understandings and sensibilities in an assorted array of approaches — but it all leads to a better understanding of the photographs and the social factors which shape their imagery and ideas. The following "black and white" portfolio represents a small group of contemporary photographers in Hawaii whose concerns exemplify the interpretations and reportage of their Hawaiian-Japanese-American experience — an experience which is portrayed by their own personal observations during interactions with the community in which they live. They are extensions of the self and they reveal that self in ways that other media do not. It is evident that they strive to produce works with enduring elements of structure and meaning, and to lay ground for photography as a medium for creative pursuit. Together, these photographers and their works give call to the emergence of a new wave of Japanese-Americans in Hawaii.

—Shuzo Uemoto

The black and white images in this formal photographic portfolio (pages 110–125) were captured in local light by four of Hawaii's finest photo artists — Shuzo Uemoto, Stan Tomita, Paul Kodama and Frank Salmoiraghi. In keeping with the gallery formats in which their work is usually displayed, each print is titled and signed.

Lester. Iwalei Series   Shuzo Uemoto

S. Tomita . Masskuc   [signature]

Cherry Pink, Mrs. Eiko Yorita

Hokassi's New Wave

115

maakua waterfall, hawaii, 1977

hubris, queen's bath, hawaii. 1973

a portrait of m.j. , hawaii . 1980

MRS. Kikuyo Saiki, waipahu, hawaii, 1973

white ROCK , in homage to sengai , hawaii , 1982

120

hatsugama, hawaii, 1978

121

SERIES: Summer Ritual 198~

Paul K. Kodama

SERIES: summer Ritual 198~   Paul. K. Koikma

Keohi Nakazawa, Waipio Valley - 1974

Salmoiraghi

Toma Bakery, Pahoa - 1976   Salmoiraghi

125

MORE DREAMS REALIZED

THE HEALING KINGDOM

<u>words of an old poet</u>

Only in books have I seen
the waves of Hokusai,
his views of Fujiyama,
the beautiful white-crested mountain.
Yet I can feel
the rocking of the boats on his ocean,
the world pulling me forward to a new place.
But my nostalgia for health pulls me back,
beckons me to rest awhile in a small bay,
where I would see nothing of the world's cities,
where nothing would fill my view
but thatched houses, tall trees,
and Fujiyama,
rising through the clouds.
Only in books have I seen these things,
yet I wait,
hoping those waves will one day find me,
a willing passenger
and completely restored
to good health.

—Pat Matsueda

Summer and Melody Onishi wear *furisode kimono* for recitals at the Hanayagi Dancing Academy, where they study classical and modern Japanese dance. Preceding pages: the main altar of the Maui Jinsha Shinto Shrine was built for $5,000 in 1917. After World War II the shrine was moved from Kahului to Paukukalo.

One thousand immigrants each gave a dollar to build the worship hall of the Maui Jinsha Shinto Shrine. Their names are on this "Thousand Horses" painting. During World War II, the rising sun flags of Japan were painted white. At left: the Buddha of Western Paradise glows over the Byodo-in Temple in Kaneohe, Oahu.

131

Clayton Amemiya is a *sansei* potter and farmer in Waiakeauka, where he lives with his family in the hills above Hilo. When he's not working with his wood-fired kiln, he farms dryland *taro (dasheen)* and limes. His grandparents came to Hawaii in 1907 from Niigata (his mother's side) and Yamanashi, Japan, to work for Waialua Sugar Co. His parents also worked for the plantations, as did one of his brothers. Another brother is an attorney and his four sisters are housewives on the Mainland.

Alan Tokunaga grew up in Sprecklesville, Maui. When he left in the mid-60s to study astronomy on the Mainland, Mauna Kea was bare of observatories. Tokunaga returned home with a Ph.D. and became the staff astronomer for the University of Hawaii's observatory on the Big Island's clear and heady peak.

The first 26 Okinawans arrived in 1900. Today there are more than 40,000 and they have preserved Okinawa's unique traditions and dance, which these ladies from the Lanakila Senior Center share at the annual United Okinawan Association Festival.

134

Aloha Week in September attracts floral floats, bands and military units from around the world, including Japan, which sent the Shinto's *mikoshi katsugi-ninsoku*, the men who carry the shrines down Waikiki's Kalakaua Avenue for the annual parade.

The Manoa Japanese Language School is home for Manoa Aikido, whose *sensei* is Masagi Yamashita. At left: Hanae Miura came to Hawaii in 1975 to demonstrate *naginata,* the Japanese martial art for women. She was asked to stay and teach men, women and children how to use the 7-foot-long sword.

Mitsutaro and Fuji Hamamoto settled on the Garden Island of Kauai, where they were buried in the Koloa Church cemetery. The old store fronts of Koloa have been renovated and the plantation town is now a museum and tourist attraction. At right: the bodies of Japanese immigrants are buried in cemeteries throughout Hawaii. At Alae, below Mauna Kea, Big Island immigrants buried their loved ones in a graveyard surrounded by a field of sugar cane and sometimes snowcapped mountains.

Sake, Sweet Sake!

Like the pale carpet of *Aspergillus oryzae* that creeps along every grain of rice in the brewer's mold bins, *sake* has permeated the Japanese experience in Hawaii. It was there at the end of an exhausting day in the cane fields, at the celebration attending the birth of a child, at the moment respects were paid to a countryman whose final resting place was 6,000 miles from home. *Sake* brought a respite from daily cares, it brought laughter and hope. In the words of Takao Nihei, whose *sake* is enjoyed by thousands of people in Hawaii every day, "The story of *sake* and the immigrants is a century-long love affair."

The first written record of *sake* in the Islands appears in documents recording the visit of the Japanese warship *Tsukuba* to Honolulu in 1876. Blue Laws were in effect at the time which prohibited the sale of liquor to Hawaiians, and the captain was dismayed to learn that he would not be able to serve *sake* to representatives of the Monarchy invited aboard for a reception. Urgent diplomatic negotiations ensued, and a one-day exception was granted to what was, in fact, a very poorly-observed rule.

On February 8, 1885 the first group of contract laborers from Japan arrived in Hawaii. They had lamented bitterly while en route about the lack of *sake*, and so they were delighted to discover that King Kalakaua had prepared a very special welcome. To the victors of a dockside *sumo* tournament went ten barrels of *sake*, probably laid on board by Robert W. Irwin, Hawaii's consul in Japan. The media and guests in the grandstands also sampled this exotic brew from the East and proclaimed it a fine beverage, "not 'catlap'

Takao Nihei became brewmaster of the Honolulu Sake Brewery in 1954.

at any rate."

The happy promise of the immigrants' first day in Hawaii was not fulfilled by the grim life they encountered on the plantations, where conditions were not far removed from slavery. Like disillusioned men everywhere, they sought solace in drink, but good drink was not to be found. There was only *okolehao* or the bootleg sold by Chinese peddlers. As drinking and gambling spread in the camps, the immigrants' wives grew concerned, and when they learned that a shipment of *sake* was en route to Honolulu from a benefactor in Japan they approached a prohibitionist minister named Kanichi Miyama to intervene. An 1887 newspaper clipping shows Miyama in action, emptying a barrel of *sake* into a Honolulu gutter while a shocked *okusan* protects her nostrils from the liquor's noxious assault with a demurely raised hand.

It was a bitter blow for the *sake* lovers of Hawaii, and a great victory for the minister, who went on to gain many converts among the immigrant wives and ended up as the leader of the temperance movement in Japan.

Fortunately common sense and market forces soon prevailed, and by 1893 *sake* was readily available in Hawaii as a luxury Japanese import. Though the monthly wage for a sugar worker was only $15, sales increased until in 1898 the per capita consumption of *sake* was 72 gallons a year. This works out to a little over three cups a day for every Japanese in the Islands, a preposterous figure; apparently Hawaii's other ethnic groups were also finding *sake* much to their liking.

In 1908 imported *sake* was selling at $2.25 a gallon, but an enterprising immigrant from Hiroshima named Tajiro Sumida figured he could get the price down to under $1.50 if *sake* were brewed in Hawaii. With a *hui* of investors he established the Honolulu Sake Brewery on September 3, 1908, and by December of that year the immigrants were sampling the first *sake* to ever be brewed outside Japan. The concensus at the time was that *sake* brewing was best left to experts in the motherland, for in Hawaii's warm climate the *sake* soon spoiled and had to be returned to the brewery.

Brewmasters brought in from Japan couldn't solve the spoilage problem, and a distraught Sumida watched his capital dwindle away and suffered the painful indignity of having to lay off workers. It was at this desperate juncture that inspiration struck and Sumida installed refrigeration in the fermentation area in an effort to duplicate ideal cold-weather *sake* brewing conditions. He also began to import lactic acid, which just months earlier had been found to greatly safeguard the *sake* brewing process. In two swift strokes Sumida had solved the basic problems entailed in making *sake* in a tropical climate.

Financially he was home free, and when Prohibition closed the brewery in 1920 he was the most successful Japanese businessman in Hawaii, with an annual profit of $56,000 on sales of over a million gallons of *sake* a year. He had brought the price of *sake* down to under a dollar a gallon and established the first major Japanese-owned industry in Hawaii. Sumida went on to found the Honolulu Japanese Chamber of Commerce and entertained prime ministers and other high officials from Japan during their visits to Hawaii.

The lifting of Prohibition in 1933 ushered in the Golden Age of *sake* in Hawaii as six breweries with a total capacity of over 5.6 million gallons a year produced such brands as Takara Masamune, Fuji Masamune and Tokyo Masamune. World War II brought a temporary shutdown but by 1947 the Honolulu Sake Brewery was again operating at full capacity, as it has continued to do down to the present day. Of 18 *sake* breweries started up by Japanese immigrants in the United States during the last 80 years it is the only remaining one.

Honolulu's *sake* is better today than ever before—the editor of Japan's prestigious *Sake* magazine once called it "a superb *sake*, dry and light with a uniquely refreshing bite." The peaceful brewery where it is made at the mouth of Pauoa Valley is visited every year by dozens of Japan's most respected brewmasters, all of whom employ fermentation technology developed in Hawaii and now used throughout the industry. It was the *sake* pioneers of Hawaii who first used refrigeration, first used stainless steel, first developed a method to brew *sake* year-round, first extended an 8-hour work day to brewery workers, and first developed techniques for brewing *sake* from California rice. A mutant strain of yeast isolated twenty years ago by Nihei, the present brewmaster, has revolutionized *sake* brewing in Japan. At one point, the Honolulu Sake Brewery was even producing a carbonated sparkling *sake* called Polynesian Champagne. In the last 100 years no brewery has contributed more to the *sake*-brewer's art than the Honolulu Sake Brewery.

— Chris Pearce

When Walter Asari was growing up on the Honolulu waterfront, his fisherman father, Kuniyoshi "James" Asari, didn't expect him to ask questions. He expected him to pay attention. That was the way he had learned the fishing business in his native Japan, and it was the path that he expected his son to follow. The Asaris were only one of hundreds of families that had come to Hawaii from the coastal areas of Wakayama Prefecture, and with them they had brought very traditional fishing skills and social attitudes.

So it was that when Walter was old enough to go to high school that he spent his summers as a cook on his father's Honolulu *aku* (skipjack tuna) boat learning the family trade. Asari, 51 recalled that as the lowest ranking member of the crew he cooked all the meals, caught fish, washed the crew's uniforms and unloaded fish from the hold.

"Even if we had a big catch and were unloading thirty to forty thousand pounds (of *aku*), and the hold was full of fish, one person had to throw it up on deck. When I was doing it, nobody would think of helping me. They were really strict. In fact, the old-timers would stand on the dock and tell me to hurry it up."

But Asari said that he knew that he had it easier than the young cooks in his father's day. Because even if his father wouldn't tell him what was going on, his fellow crew members would. This was a big advantage because in the old days, in Japan, "the old fishermen wouldn't tell you anything. If you made a mistake the bamboo poles would come out flying".

"They (old-timers) learned it all by themselves and had to be pretty observant. Right now we have Loran (ra-

dar). They learned how to use mountains as landmarks so they could find their position, and before there were depth recorders they would just go to a spot and say 'this is the place'."

There were other unofficial rules that had to be followed as well. Asari said that in his father's day, no pork could be brought on board a fishing boat, only fish and vegetables were allowed to be eaten, no women were allowed under any circumstances, and no matter how drunk or how bad a hangover a fisherman might have from the night before, he was expected to be on board when the boat left the harbor.

Asari's father had come to Honolulu at the suggestion of an uncle, and he immediately joined the small group of Wakayama fishermen who formed the core of Oahu's pre-war *aku* fleet. The *aku* were said to be larger than the *shibi* in his native Wakayama and easier to catch. The fish were plentiful and by working on a boat it was easy to save money. In short, he was told that Honolulu was a place where a young Japanese could get ahead.

In time, Kuniyoshi did. He saved his money and with the support of friends was eventually able to buy a 75 foot sampan, the *Tenjin Maru*. Business sailed along in those early years, but when Japan attacked Pearl Harbor in 1941, all of the vessels belonging to Japanese resident aliens were confiscated by the military. The Asari family was not compensated for their sampan, which at that time was valued at $20,000 (or approximately $130,000 in 1985 dollars). In addition, because Asari's father was not a citizen, he was not permitted to go fishing again until the war ended. Asari said he went back to fishing anyway, but he could no

longer be a boat owner. Now he had to work for somebody else.

Before World War II, nearly 80 percent of Hawaii's fishing fleet was Japanese. Fishing was Hawaii's third largest industry and the tuna catch alone brought in $1.2 million in the year 1940 to 1941 and employed more than 2,000 people. Newspapers of the period carried stories promoting the growth of the industry and optimistic projections of the future, but all of this changed with the attack on Pearl Harbor.

Ernest Steiner, who was assistant fishing coordinator here from 1941 to 1943, remembers that the Army or Coast Guard had a general rule to remove all Japanese fishing boats away from the waterfront. "They couldn't investigate each person," he said, because "they had a lot of boats". Steiner recalls that boats from several parts of Oahu were confiscated. Larger *aku* boats were taken to Pearl Harbor and smaller *akule* (big-eyed scad) and dragline boats were hauled up the Ala Wai. There was, however, some form of compensation for some of the boats. One boat owner of the period, Captain Naboru Tsue, 72, was able to sell his *aku* boat at the beginning of the war as a supply boat for the Kalaupapa settlement.

But for other Japanese boat owners such as Kuniyoshi Asari, the war was a financial disaster. He and others lost both their boats and their livelihoods, and the adverse effects on Hawaii's fishing industry were immediate. From a pre-war high of 19.4 million pounds in 1940, the amount of fish caught here dropped to 3.5 million pounds by 1945.

There were newspaper articles written toward the end of the war that both encouraged the "revitalization of the industry" and predicted that the industry would never recover. After the war some of the sons of fishing people left their boats and took other kinds of jobs, but others, such as Tsue and Kuniyoshi saw opportunity: they realized that fish were still abundant out at sea, that the war had created a strong demand for fresh fish, and that many of the older but still reliable boats were still sitting unused and waiting.

Asari recalls that his father immediately went back to fishing and in time was able to see his son take command of his own boat. He said his father took the loss of his boat during the war philosophically—in a manner worthy of his ancestors. "My dad took it in stride. He said it happened and it couldn't be helped. A boat could be replaced, but keeping the family together was the main thing. He said as long as he had his family he had nothing to gripe about . . . ."

Postcript: Hawaii's once prosperous *aku* fleet has fallen upon hard times. Catch rates have fallen steadily since the days when Walter Asari first went to sea. Indeed, in the last five years *aku* catches have dropped by more than fifty percent. The lower catch rates and the advanced age of the boats in the fleet (the average is 57 years) have made it increasingly difficult for fishermen to make a living. Since 1948, the number of *aku* boats has dropped from 32 to 12. There are indications that this fleet number may continue to decrease. The recent closure of the Honolulu cannery has made it more difficult for *aku* fishermen to sell their extra catch during the peak season and has caused the price that they get for their fish to drop. University of Hawaii researchers believe that there will be an *aku* fleet for some years to come; but that if present economic conditions continue it will grow progressively smaller.

—Mike Markrich

An auctioneer at Suisan Fish Auction Market in Hilo checks the day's catch.

Moiliili Musings

Once in a while, Seemingly
out of nowhere — particularly
when the shadows lie long, I
am overwhelmed with a yearning
to touch again an essential
core of my beginning, the
rudiments of my mathematics,
which is being Japanese — so
long a personal battlefield,
finally resolved, The burden
of growing up brown in a
prevailing white society, The
burden of growing up World
War II, its unrelenting
message that being Japanese
is Un-American and
Un-American is bad.
I learned how to "rise above it."
(Whiter than white.)

But one's core, like the
genetic code, refuses to be
denied; keeps asserting itself.

Finally, joyfully, the battle
is past, the guilts dismantled,
the self restored,
the servant gone.

So now when the yearning
comes I rejoice in the passion
of this soulful primal call
to celebrate I'm Japanese
And share green tea with
a special friend, Or envelope
myself in elegant splendor
a lavish heirloom *kimono*,
my mother's artistry, Or
mold a clay pot, Paint a
blurry watercolor, Write
a quiet poem. And sometimes
when there is a trembling,
I celebrate by seeking out
remnants of old Japanese
neighborhoods for communion.

Moiliili is my particular favorite.

It lies at the foot of the University of Hawaii's Manoa campus, pressed by Waikiki on the other side. It is a high density area with mostly low and medium rise apartment dwellings.

The population, once overwhelmingly Japanese, now reflects a mix, including new Southeast Asian immigrants. But the dominant group is still Japanese, with a high rate of working mothers. Hence, child care and enrichment programs for children are available year-round.

Moiliili was once a marshland of duck ponds, lotus farms and rice fields. Historical literature states that Queen Kamamalu, King Kam II's bride and half-sister, had her summer cottage on the banks of Kapaakea Springs where the Willows Restaurant now sits.

It is said the Chinese who moved out of the plantations first set up shop there to serve the Japanese and Chinese farmers and laborers from the nearby stone quarry. These shopkeepers later moved on for bigger stakes and the Japanese took over.

The businesses changed, of course, over the years. Among old favorites now gone are Charley's Tavern, the cracked seed store that sat across from the Varsity Theater, the old Honolulu Stadium, where Babe Ruth slugged a homerun in 1934, several flower shops, and Kuhio Grill, a gathering spot that was priced right for collegians and locals for some 30 years.

The Kuhio Grill's owner, the late Mark Miyashiro, warmly known to customers as Miya-san, was an angel to many-a-struggling art student, including the following who went on to become well-known Island artists: Tadashi Sato, Bumpei Akaji, Satoru Abe

and the late Bob Ochikubo. Their work adorned Miyashiro's weathered pub and gave rise to the nickname Kuhio Gallery and Grill.

In many cases, the old places have been replaced by the plastic nightmare of fast food and all-night groceries.

But despite all that, there is still enough of the old charm left in the straggly stretch of buildings along King Street to retain the Moiliili flavor.

The community, with the vital force of the Moiliili Community Center, Moiliili Hongwanji and the Church of the Crossroads, remains a hometown classic for Hawaii's *issei* and *nisei*.

And here are some of the things that

continue to make Moiliili such an ethnic celebration for me:

— There's always some sort of Japanese cultural enrichment class I can take at the community center—from flower arranging to *sushi* making and Japanese language classes.

— During the summer, the center is the site for the Moiliili Hongwanji's colorful *bon* dances in honor of the dead. This folk event evokes fond childhood memories of wearing new *kimono* with fancy sashes and lacquer heel slippers with bells in them. I recall waking up the next morning, thinking I had had the best time I ever had.

— Another fun offering at the center is the thrift shop operated by the seniors. It is so tidy it's easy hunting for bargains. I have found some wonderful nostalgia treasures there.

— Like any "local," I love slurping strawberry shaved ice with ice cream and Japanese *azuki* beans on a warm day. The Goodie Goodie Drive-in and several other little places carry good ones. I equally love slurping on a steaming bowl of *saimin* with meatsticks on a cold evening at the small diners scattered about.

— Several other Japanese "local out" snacks are sold at the *mochi* (rice cake) store. The shop is fun but the woman operator isn't. She's on the hard-boiled side. She serves to point up an important fact: that not all Japanese bow and smile all the time. There are grouches, too. At any rate, what I love to do is to get sacks full of freshly roasted *shoyu* peanuts, pink and green pinched *mochi*, rice crackers *(senbei)* and cracked seed. And then start munching. (Lucky for me, my mother never learned how often I spent all my lunch money on cracked seed during my barefoot, pigtail days in Pahoa on the Big Island.)

— I enjoy fabrics and a wonderful indulgence for me is to spend an hour or two at Kuni Dry Goods to browse and feel the assembly of fabrics, racks of buttons and trimmings and then go through a pile of pattern books, fantasizing. Most Japanese women love to sew. So do I. My appreciation for fabrics and design comes from my mother, whose sense of taste, artistry, craft and sheer grit was and is a continuing source of inspiration. Our parlor was a gathering place where salesmen brought their finery. Mom helped the ladies make their selections. She sewed the fancy *kimono,* and I often sat beside her, sewing my dolls' clothes. On special occasions, the women in the village came again to our parlor so Mom could help them get dressed. I used to enjoy watching all this fussing going on. The saleswomen at Kuni's convey this same love of texture and design.

— Another Moiliili treat are the flower shops along King Street. Several of the old ones are gone. The first florists opened there because just beyond, in neighboring Manoa, was where the flowers grew for acres and acres before they were uprooted to make way for University of Hawaii buildings and dormitories.

Every time I go to the Moiliili Post Office — among the smallest and sweetest—I make a point of pausing at the florists to absorb the bombardment of color and perfume. It's the next best thing to visiting the family-tended Valentine gardens in Manoa.

— Occasionally, I like to stop at the Moiliili Hongwanji to sit and meditate. Before the ornate altar I find a peace this is curiously different from that in a Catholic Church. Much more do-it-yourself, open-ended, unexpected.

The Moiliili Store, which is a must for stocking up on dried squid, dried fish (small ones with heads and tails still on), French fried peas and Hilo brand saloon pilot and soda crackers. The best. My favorite plantation special is to smear the crackers with Best Foods mayonnaise. A close second is drippy condensed milk, soft fresh dairy butter, or, for a *haole* mood, peanut butter and orange marmalade. In the back section are vats of pickled Japanese veggies, wonderful scallions and preserved plums (*ume boshi* with *chiso*—wonderful stuff) for *chazuke* (tea and rice). There's also a steamer of hot *laulau* and freshly sliced fish and octopus *sashimi*.

Fukuya, Moiliili's popular *okazu-ya* (deli), which is a stop I make only with the clear intention of pigging-out on a Japanese plate lunch.

And so, while squid and *mochi*
are part of the fabric of
being Japanese, the joy of
Moiliili for me is touching
the people. Exchanging quiet
smiles with Moiliili ladies,
carefully permed in their
sensible dresses (and slacks),
menfolk in their everyday
inscrutableness and the
occasional heavily made-up
"sushi girl" with fake lashes.
I feel at home in the music of
their interchange. Language,
like wind chime calligraphies,
giggles bouncing off a
mountain brook. I feel such
gladness unfold.

— Tomi Kaizawa Knaefler

145

HISTORICAL CHRONOLOGY

1258 — Typhoons blow Asian fishermen across the Pacific, and shipwrecked crews, believed to be Japanese, land twice at Makapu'u Point. No one knows what happened to the men.

1270 — A storm-battered *sampan,* filled with a cargo of sugar and drifting with its Japanese crew, arrives at Kahului, Maui. The sugar is planted and the crew become Islanders.

1804 — The first recorded Japanese arrive in Hawaii. Tsudayu, a 61-year-old shipwrecked sailor and three crew are picked up by the *Nadejida,* a Russian ship, and put upon Oahu's shore. Tsudayu writes "Hawaii Kenbun Raku." During the next 60 years, scores of Japanese sailors, drifting in the sea, would be rescued by whalers and cargo ships, and dropped off in Hawaii. Some stayed; others returned home.

1860 — Japan's Embassy to the United States arrives in Honolulu unexpectedly. Their American escort ship needs coal and the envoys, though *lu'au*-ed for two weeks before they leave, are unwilling to sign a treaty of amity with the Kingdom.

1868 — The first group of Japanese laborers — the Gannen Mono — arrive May 17 without their government's permission to leave Japan. There are 146 men, five women and two children in this group.

1869 — The laborers are treated poorly and their sad reports reach Japan. The Imperial government sends a delegation to Honolulu to investigate labor conditions. Forty immigrants return to Japan. An amity treaty between the kingdoms is ratified in 1871.

1881 — King Kalakaua visits Japan during his world tour and asks the government to permit emigration to Hawai'i. He proposes a marriage between his niece, Princess Kaiulani, and a Japanese prince. The proposal is politely declined.

1885 — Immigration from Japan resumes and a first shipload of 943 laborers, with contracts to work on the plantations, arrive Feb. 8 on board the *City of Tokio.* King Kalakaua and the Hawaiian people greet their Asian brothers and sisters with *aloha.* The Japanese respond with demonstrations of *sumo*-wrestling and *kendo* swordplay, and are invited to 'Iolani Palace. Work at some plantations was cruel and within a month Japanese laborers stopped working at Paia, Maui.

1892 — Onome Bunichi starts the first Japanese language newspaper, *The Nippon Shuho.*

1893 — The warship *Naniwa* arrives to protect Japanese nationals after the Kingdom of Hawai'i is overthrown.

1894 — The last shipload of government-contracted laborers arrives. In nine years, 26 ships brought about 29,000 laborers. The first Buddhist sect — the Jodos — arrive, followed in 1897 by the Higashi and Honpa Hongwanji; the Nichiren, 1900; Soto, 1903; and Shingon, in 1914. By 1908, there were 33 shrines and temples and 26 Christian churches.

1896 — Rev. Takie Okumura, a Christian minister, starts the first Japanese language school. Suspicious *haoles* saw the schools as "hotbeds of un-Christian and un-American propaganda." By 1919, there were 163 Japanese language schools.

1899 — Gorokichi Nakasuji revolutionizes the tuna industry with a new boat that is 32-feet-long and 5.8-feet-wide. The fishing industry thrives.

1900 — The first Okinawans, 26 of them, arrive in Hawaii. By 1911, there were about 12,000.

1904 — The first organized labor strike by Japanese closes the Waipahu plantation for a week.

1905 — The first all Japanese baseball team, the Asahi, is established. In Lahaina, 1,400 plantation workers enter into a labor strike.

1907 — Picture brides start arriving. More than 14,000 come to Hawaii in the next 16 years. Most stayed; some, dissatisfied with the Islands, return home to their families.

1909 — Some 5,000 Japanese sugar workers on Oahu strike for higher wages. Workers are evicted from their homes. Strike leaders Yasutaro Soga, Yokichi Tasaka, Keitaro Kawamura, Fred Makino and Motoyuki Negoro are jailed by government using "emergency powers." The strike is broken, but plantations improve conditions.

1910 — Japanese now form the largest ethnic group in Hawaii, accounting for 79,663 people or 40 percent of the population of 191,909. There are 140 language schools with 7,000 students.

1917 — The United States enters World

Arata Inouye of Haiku, Maui (left), in his U.S. Army uniform in 1918.

War I. About 29,000 Japanese—citizens and non-citizens—sign up for the draft and a Japanese "D Company" is organized as part of the Hawaii National Guard, but is not sent off to battle.

1919—A Federation of Japanese Labor in Hawaii is formed to work for better wages.

1920—Oahu sugar workers—4,000 Japanese and 2,000 Filipinos—strike again for higher wages. 12,000 people are evicted from their homes. The walkout costs the Japanese $200,000; the plantations, $12 million. It ends without success seven months later, but working conditions and salaries are improved.

1920—Kauai's James T. Hamada is the first American of Japanese Ancestry (AJA) to run for the Territorial House of Representatives. He loses in the Republican primary.

1924—The U.S. Congress enacts a Japanese Exclusion Law, barring Japanese immigration.

1930—Andy M. Yamashiro of Honolulu and Tasaku Oka are the first Americans of Japanese Ancestry elected to the Territorial House. Noboru Miyake of Kauai is the first to be elected to a county Board of Supervisors. There are 414 *nisei* teachers in public schools.

1931—1,300 Japanese families are growing coffee in Kona on the Big Island of Hawaii.

1935—The 50th anniversary of the arrival of contract laborers is celebrated. A congressional subcommittee arrives from Washington, D.C., to hold statehood hearings for Hawaii.

1939—Isami Doi, an artist from Kauai, wins the prestigious Palace of Legion of Honor—the first oriental to ever earn such an award.

1941—The Japanese armed forces attack Pearl Harbor on Dec. 7. Hawaii's Japanese language schools are closed; martial law is declared nine hours after the attack. The FBI rounds up priests, language school officials and fishermen. Eventually, 1,444 leaders of the Japanese community are sent to internment camps. Four days later, 517 *nisei* in the Territorial Guard are discharged without explanation. They reapply and form the 34th Combat Engineer Regiment, a labor battalion.

1943—The 442nd Regimental Combat Team is organized with 9,500 volunteers, 3,000 of whom are taken. The unit is composed of Japanese from Hawaii and the mainland and trains at Camp Shelby. The 100th Infantry Battalion, organized earlier, trains at Camp McCoy, Wis. The 100th is the first to enter the combat zone, landing in North Africa on Sept. 2. During the war, the 442nd/100th would be the Army's most decorated and decimated American unit: 3,506 wounded, 67 missing, 569 killed, 81 dead from wounds and 177 injured in action.

1945—Atom bombs explode on Hiroshima, ancestral home of many of Hawaii's Japanese, and Nagasaki. The war ends. Many Japanese veterans take advantage of the GI Bill of Rights to further their education.

1954—Democrats, with the help of *nisei* candidates, gain control of the Territorial Legislature.

1959—Hawaii becomes a state. Wilfred C. Tsukiyama becomes the first AJA to be named a Chief Justice and Dan Inouye the first Hawaii AJA to be elected to Congress.

1962—Inouye is sworn in as the first AJA to be elected to the U.S. Senate.

1964—Shunichi Kimura of Hawaii County is the first AJA to be elected a mayor in the state. Jesse Kuhaulua, 6-foot, 4-inches and 430 pounds, goes to Japan to become a *sumo* wrestler, and during his 21 year career, "Takamiyama" (High View Mountain) wrestles 1,654 bouts (1,431 consecutively) and breaks all records. In 1972, he wins the Emperor's Cup, the first non-Japanese citizen to do so.

1971—Politician Matsuo Takabuki is the first AJA to be named a trustee of the Bishop Estate.

1974—George Ariyoshi becomes the first AJA governor in the nation and is re-elected in 1978 and 1982.

1975—Hawaii's Japanese community greets the Emperor and Empress of Japan, who stop in Hawaii enroute home from a visit to the Mainland United States.

1978—An Air Force officer, Maj. Ellison Onizuka of Kealakekua, Kona, is the first AJA to be named an astronaut.

1985—Onizuka completes a secret space flight on board *Skylab*—Jan. 24 to Jan. 27—and Hawaii joins its Japanese community in a grand Centennial celebration of the arrival of the first Kanyaku Imin.

The "Japanese" baseball team posed for this studio portrait about 1917.

BIBLIOGRAPHY

Books

Adams, Romanzo Colfax. *The Japanese in Hawaii: A Statistical Study Bearing on the Future Number and Voting Strength and on the Economic and Social Character of the Hawaiian Japanese.* New York: National Committee on American Japanese Relations, 1924.

Allen, Gwenfread. *Hawaii's War Years, 1941–1945.* Honolulu: University of Hawaii Press, 1950.

Aller, Curtis Cosmos, Jr. *Labor Relations in the Hawaiian Sugar Industry.* Berkeley: Institute of Industrial Relations, University of California, 1957.

_____. "The Evolution of Hawaiian Labor Relations: From Benevolent Paternalism to Mature Collective Bargaining." Ph.D. thesis [Political Economy and Government], Harvard University, 1958.

Beekman, Allan. *Hawaiian Tales.* Detroit: Harlo Press, 1970.

Bushnell, O. A. *Stone of Kannon.* Honolulu: University of Hawaii Press, 1979.

Coman, Katherine. *The History of Contract Labor in the Hawaiian Islands.* New York: American Economic Association, 1903.

Conroy, Hilary. *The Japanese Frontier in Hawaii, 1868–1898.* Berkeley and Los Angeles: University of California Press, 1953.

_____, and T. Scott Miyakawa, eds. *East Across the Pacific: Historical and Sociological Studies of Japanese Immigration and Assimilation.* Santa Barbara and Oxford: American Bibliographical Center CLIO Press, 1972.

Daws, Gavan. *Shoal of Time; A History of the Hawaiian Islands.* New York: The Macmillan Company, 1968.

Day, A. Grove. *Hawaii and Its People,* rev. ed. New York: Meredith Press, 1968.

DeFrancis, John, with V. R. Lincoln. *Things Japanese in Hawaii.* Honolulu: University of Hawaii Press, 1973.

Fuchs, Lawrence H. *Hawaii Pono: A Social History.* New York: Harcourt, Brace and World, 1961.

Goto, Yasuo Baron. *Children of Gan-Nen-Mono: The First-Year Men.* Honolulu: The Bishop Museum Press, 1968.

Hawaii's Laborers' Association. *Facts About the Strike on Sugar Plantations in Hawaii.* Honolulu, 1920.

Hongo, Bob Nobuyuki. *Hey, Pineapple.* Tokyo? Printed by the Hokuseido Press; stamped: Distributed by International Traders, Honolulu, Hawaii, 1958.

Ichihashi, Yamato. *Japanese in the United States: A Critical Study of the Problems of the Japanese Immigrants and Their Children.* 1932. Reprinted, New York: Arno Press and *The New York Times,* 1969.

Inouye, Daniel K. with Lawrence Elliot. *Journey to Washington.* Englewood Cliffs, N. J.: Prentice-Hall, 1967.

Kuykendall, Ralph S. *Hawaii in the World War.* Honolulu: The Historical Commission, 1928.

_____, and A. Grove Day. *Hawaii: A History; From Polynesian Kingdom to American Commonwealth.* New York: Prentice-Hall, Inc., 1948.

Ladenson, Alex. "The Japanese in Hawaii." Ph.D. dissertation [History], University of Chicago, 1938.

Lind, Andrew W., *Hawaii's Japanese: An Experiment in Democracy.* Princeton: Princeton University Press, 1946.

_____. *Hawaii's People.* Honolulu: University of Hawaii Press, 1955.

_____. *The Japanese in Hawaii Under War Conditions.* Institute of Pacific Relations, American Council Paper No. 5. Honolulu, 1943.

MacDonald, Alexander. *Revolt in Paradise: The Social Revolution in Hawaii after Pearl Harbor.* New York: Stephen Dave, 1946.

Mahlmann, (Capt.) John J. *Reminiscences of an Ancient Mariner.* Yokohama, Japan: Japanese Gazette Printing Co., 1918.

Matsuda, Mitsugu. *The Japanese in Hawaii: An Annotated Bibliography of Japanese Americans.* Honolulu: University of Hawaii Press, Social Sciences and Linguistics Institute, Series No. 5, 1975.

Murphy, Thomas D. *Ambassadors in Arms: The Story of Hawaii's 100th Battalion.* Honolulu: University of Hawaii Press, 1954.

Norbeck, Edward. *Pineapple Town, Hawaii.* Berkeley: University of California Press, 1959.

Odo, Franklin. *The Pictorial History of Japanese in Hawaii: 1885–1924.* Honolulu: Bishop Museum Press, 1985.

Ogawa, Dennis M. *Jan Ken Po: The World of Hawaii's Japanese Americans.* Honolulu: Japanese American Research Center, 1973.

_____, and Glen Grant. *Tengoku.* Honolulu: Mutual Publishing Co., 1985.

Platt, Sanford L. *Immigration and Emigration in the Hawaiian Sugar Industry.* Honolulu: Hawaiian Sugar Planter's Association, 1950.

Rademaker, John A. *These are Americans: The Japanese Americans in Hawaii in World War II.* Palo Alto, California: Pacific Books, 1951.

Richstad, Jim Andrew. "The Press and the Courts Under Martial Law in Hawaii During World War II — From Pearl Harbor to Duncan V. Kahanamoku." Ph. D. dissertation [Journalism], University of Minnesota, 1967.

Saiki, Patsy. *Japanese Women in Hawaii: 100 Years of History.* Honolulu: Kisaku, Inc., 1985.

Sakamaki, Shunzō. "A History of the Japanese Press in Hawaii." Master's thesis [History], University of Hawaii, 1928.

Shirey, Orville C. *Americans: The Story of the 442d Combat Team.* 1st ed. Washington: Infantry Journal Press, 1946.

Shirota, Jon H. *Lucky Come Hawaii.* New York: Bantam Books, 1965.

_____. *Pineapple White.* Los Angeles: Ohara Publications, Inc., 1972.

Strona, Proserfina A. *Japanese in Hawaii: A bibliography.* Honolulu: Hawaii and Pacific Unit, State Library Branch, 1974.

Tajima, Paul J. "Japanese Buddhism in Hawaii: Its Background, Origin, and Adaptation to Local Conditions." Master's thesis [Asian Studies], University of Hawaii, 1935.

Toyama, Tetsuo. *Eighty Years in Hawaii.* Tokyo: Tosho Printing Co., 1971. Text in English and Japanese.

Tsutsumi, Takashi. "History of Hawaii Laborers' Movement." Translated from the Japanese by Umetaro Okumura. Honolulu: Hawaii Sugar Planter's Association, 1922.

United Japanese Society of Hawaii. *History of Japanese in Hawaii,* edited by James H. Okahata. Honolulu: United Japanese Society of Hawaii, 1971.

Wakukawa, Ernest K. *A History of the Japanese People in Hawaii.* Honolulu: The Toyo Shoin, 1938.

Watanabe, Shinichi. "Diplomatic Relations Between the Hawaiian Kingdom and the Empire of Japan, 1860 – 1893." Master's thesis [History], University of Hawaii, 1944.

Weinberg, Daniel Erwin. "The Movement to 'Americanize' the Japanese Community in Hawaii: An Analysis of the One Hundred Percent Americanization Activity in the Territory of Hawaii as Expressed in the Caucasian Press, 1919 – 1923." Master's thesis [History], University of Hawaii, 1967.

White, James E. "The Japanese of Hawaii, 1941 – 1945." Master's thesis [History], University of Chicago, 1950.

Articles

Adams, Romanzo Colfax. "Some Statistics on the Japanese in Hawaii." *Foreign Affairs* 2(1923): 310 – 318.

_____. "Japanese Migration Statistics." *Sociology and Social Research* 13(1929): 436 – 445.

Baker, Ray Stannard. "Human Nature in Hawaii." *The American Magazine* 73(1912): 328 – 339.

Beekman, Take, and Allan Beekman. "Hawaii's Great Japanese Strike; Opposed to the Struggle of the Japanese for Equality and Dignity was the Combined Might of Hawaii's Government and Industry." *Pacific Citizen* 51(1960): B1 – B8.

Bishop, Sereno Edwards. "Brief History of Differences Between Hawaii and Japan." In *Hawaiian Almanac and Annual for 1898,* pp. 70 – 75. Honolulu: Thomas G. Thrum, 1898.

Bogardus, Emory S. "The Japanese in Hawaii." *Sociology and Social Research* 19(1935): 562 – 569.

Bouslog, Harriet, and Myer C. Symonds. "Memorandum on History of Labor and the Law in Territory of Hawaii." [*Hearings on*] *Civil [Cases], No. 828 and No. 836.* United States District Court for the District of Hawaii. Mimeographed. Honolulu, 1948.

Burlingame, Burl. "Children of the Rising Sun." *Honolulu Star-Bulletin,* review of TV show by Bob Jones and Grant Conching, February 11, 1985.

California Joint Immigration Committee. *Congress and Japan: Inside History of the Exclusion Measure. The Fundamental Reasons Which Induced Action by Congress. The Movement to Have That Action Reconsidered.* San Francisco, 1925.

Carter, William H. "The Japanese in Hawaii." *Atlantic Monthly* 128(1921): 255 – 257.

Clark, Thomas Blake, and O. D. Russell. "Hail Our Japanese-American GIs," *Reader's Digest,* XLVII (July, 1945), 65– 67.

Conroy, Hilary. "'Asiatic Federation' and the Japanese Immigration to Hawaii." In *Fifty-Eighth Annual Report of the Hawaiian Historical Society for the Year 1949,* pp. 6– 12. Honolulu, 1950.

Crewdson, W. "Japanese Emigrants." *Nineteenth Century and After* 56(1904): 813– 819.

Desilva, Frank A. "Music is Her Thing." *Hawaii Herald,* March 18, 1971, p. 1.

"Diary Describes Voyage from Japan 100 Years Ago." *Honolulu Star-Bulletin,* June 14, 1968, p. A-10.

Fruto, Ligaya. "Japanese Arrived 100 Years Ago." *Honolulu Star-Bulletin,* January 25, 1968, p. A-9.

Gillespie, James J., and Lauren E. McBride. "The 100th Battalion (Nisei) Against the Germans," *Infantry Journal,* Overseas Edition, LV (December, 1944), pp. 8– 15.

"Hawaii's Japanese Problem." *Hawaii Educational Review* 32(1944): 236.

Hunter, Gene. "History Logs Early Voyagers." *Sunday Star-Bulletin and Advertiser,* June 16, 1968, p. D-16.

Ige, T. H. "Hawaii's Loyal Japanese." *The Nation* 155(1942): 120.

Inouye, Daniel K. "Marvel of Human Spirit." *Sunday Star-Bulletin and Advertiser,* June 16, 1968, p. D-12.

Inouye, Souno. "How the Japanese Came to the Islands. What of the Future of the Japanese?" *Honolulu Advertiser,* April 30, 1925.

"Japanese in Hawaii." *New Republic* 106(1942): 445.

"The Japanese in Hawaii: 100 Years in Progress." *Honolulu Star-Bulletin* Progress Edition, February 19, 1985.

Jones, Maude, "Naturalization of Orientals in Hawaii Prior to 1900." In *Forty-First Annual Report of the Hawaiian Historical Society for the Year 1932,* pp. 66– 69. Honolulu, 1933.

Kimura, Yukiko. Some effects of the war situation upon the alien Japanese in Hawaii. *Social Process in Hawaii.* 8:18– 28, 1943.

Kuykendall, Ralph S. *The Earliest Japanese Labor Immigration to Hawaii.* University of Hawaii Occasional Papers No. 25. Honolulu, 1935.

Lind, Andrew W. "The Changing Japanese in Hawaii." *Social Process in Hawaii* 4(1938): 37– 40.

Oshiro, Sandra. "From plantation worker to hotel owner." *Honolulu Advertiser,* February 7, 1985, p. B-1.

———. "Here from Japan, first in long line of dentists." *Honolulu Advertiser,* February 7, 1985, p. B-1, B-2.

"Pacesetters of the Pacific '85." *Honolulu Star-Bulletin,* Progress Edition, section 1, pp. 1– 36.

"Plantation Labor Trouble of 1909. Strike of Japanese Laborers on Oahu." In *Hawaiian Almanac and Annual for 1910,* pp. 123– 127. Honolulu: Thomas G. Thrum, 1910.

Sather, Jeane. "Wakayama remembers those who emigrated." *Honolulu Star Bulletin,* February 3, 1985. p. B-3

Scott, M. M. "The Japanese in These Islands." *Pacific Commercial Advertiser,* July 2, 1906. (Fiftieth anniversary issue)

Scudder, Doremus. "Hawaii's Experience with the Japanese." *Annals of the American Academy of Political and Social Science* 93(1921): 110– 115.

Shinsato, Roy M. "The Gannen Mono: Great Expectations of the Earliest Japanese Immigrants to Hawaii." *Hawaii Historical Review* 1(1965): 180– 194.

Taylor, Lois. "Aboard the S. S. City of Tokio." *Honolulu Star-Bulletin,* February 7, 1985, p. D-1.

Yamamoto, Misako. "Cultural Conflicts and Accommodations of the First and Second Generation Japanese," *Social Press in Hawaii,* IV (May, 1938), 40– 48.

Yoshinaga, Toshimi. "Japanese Buddhist Temples in Honolulu." *Social Process in Hawaii* 3(1937): 36– 42.

Yoshizawa, Emi. "A Japanese Family in Rural Hawaii," *Social Process in Hawaii,* III (May, 1937), 56– 63.

Federal Documents

U.S. Congress. House. *Importation of Japanese Laborers.* House Document 686. 56th Cong., 1st sess. Washington, 1900.

U.S. Congress. Senate. Subcommittee on Immigration. *Japanese in Hawaii.* 66th Cong., 2d sess. Washington, 1920.

War Department. Army Forces, MIDPAC (and predecessor commands). Official records on the history of the 100th Infantry Battalion and the 442d Regimental Combat Team (in HWRD):

General Staff, Organization and Training Division, G-3, and Army Ground Forces Headquarters, Army War College, Washington. Photostatic copies of documents relative to the organization of the 100th and the 442d (28 May 1942– 10 January 1943).

Narrative history of the 100th Battalion, Separate, June 1942– 7 September 1944: 2 September 1943– 11 June 1944 (Salerno to Rome).

Unit history of the 100th Battalion, Separate (copies of organization and movement orders, rosters and awards, from 31 May 1942 to 30 April 1944).

Unit history of the 100th Battalion from 1 May 1944 to 31 October 1944.

History of the 442d Regimental Combat Team, 1 February 1943– 30 April 1946, and Narrative of Events.

Japanese Newspapers and Periodicals.

The Boy. December, 1916– June, 1919. Honolulu: Makiki Christian Church.

The Citizen. June 1954– January 1970. Honolulu, Hawaii.

The Dobo. September 1900?– December 1941. Honolulu, Hawaii: Young Men's Buddhist Association.

East-West Journal. October 1, 1976 to date. Honolulu, Hawaii: East-West Journal Corp.

Hawaii Asahi Shinbun. 1913– 1928? Hilo, Hawaii.

Hawaii Herald. October 23, 1942– January 10, 1952. Honolulu, Hawaii: F. K. Makino.

Hawaii Herald. April 1, 1969– October 26, 1973. Honolulu, Hawaii: Hawaii Hochi Ltd.

The Hawaii Herald. May 16, 1980 to date. Honolulu, Hawaii: Hawaii Hochi.

Hawaii Hochi. 1912– October 22, 1942. Honolulu, Hawaii: F. K. Makino.

Hawaii Hochi. January 11, 1952 to date. Honolulu, Hawaii: F. W. Makino.

Hawaii Jiyu Shinbun. 1896– 1905. Honolulu, Hawaii.

Hawaii Mainichi. 1912– 1942. Hilo, Hawaii.

Hawaii Mainichi Shinbun. 1952– 1965. Honolulu, Hawaii: Hawaii Mainichi Shinbun Sha.

Hawaii Nichi Nichi Shinbun. 1901– 1914? Honolulu, Hawaii.

Hawaii Nippo. October 21, 1916– 1925. Honolulu, Hawaii.

Hawaii Shinbun. 1894– 1895. Honolulu, Hawaii.

Hawaii Shinpo. 1894– 1926. Honolulu, Hawaii.

Hawaii Shokumin Shinbun. 1909– 1913? Hilo, Hawaii.

Hawaii Star. March 6, 1947– 1952? Honolulu, Hawaii.

Hawaii Times. November 2, 1942 to date. Honolulu, Hawaii: Hawaii Times.

Hawaii Times. 1914. Hilo, Hawaii.

Hawaiian Japanese Daily Chronicle. 1904– 1915. Honolulu, Hawaii.

Hilo Jiho. 1905– 1907? Hilo, Hawaii.

Hilo Shinpo. 1898– 1912. Hilo, Hawaii.

Honolulu Hochi. 1892 or 1893. Honolulu, Hawaii.

Honolulu News. 1902– 1906. Honolulu, Hawaii.

Jitsugyo No Hawaii. August 1911– December 1941. Honolulu, Hawaii.

Kauai Shinpo. 1904– 1942. Lihue, Kauai.

Kauai, Shuho. 1905– 1913. Lihue, Kauai.

Kona Echo (Kona Hankyo). February 3, 1897– July 7, 1951. Holualoa and Kailua-Kona, Hawaii.

Kona Shuho (Kona Weekly). 1915– 1920. Kealakekua, Kona, Hawaii: Kona Shuho Sha.

Kosei Okinawa (Reborn Okinawa). November 1947– October 1948. Honolulu, Hawaii: Okinawa Relief and Rehabilitation Foundation.

Maui Shinbun. 1904– December 5, 1941. Wailuku, Maui: Maui Publishing Co.

The New Americans. July 1919 – Spring, 1934. Honolulu: Makiki Christian Church.

Nippu Jiji. November 1, 1905?– October 31, 1942. Honolulu, Hawaii: Nippu Jiji Sha.

Nisei in Hawaii and the Pacific. Summer 1947– Fall 1956. Honolulu.

Rakuen Jiho. January 1919– August 1939. Honolulu, Hawaii.

Shin Nippon. 1901– 1907. Honolulu, Hawaii.

Shukan Taimusu (Weekly Times). April 3, 1959– August 28, 1964. Honolulu, Hawaii.

The Yamato. 1895– 1896. Honolulu?, Hawaii.

Yamato Shinbun. 1896– 1906. Honolulu, Hawaii: Yamato Shinbun Sha.

Yoen Jino. February 2, 1921?– April 39, 1970. Honolulu, Hawaii: Yoen Jiho Sha.

Tsuruko Koide sets type the old, old fashioned way, by hand for the *Hilo Times,*
a Japanese language newspaper, which has been published for about 30 years.

154

INDEX

Immigrants in Puunene, Maui, formed the Japanese Association Drama Group about 1915. The two women in the front row are probably men, since ladies in Japan were banned from acting for moral reasons. Some men specialized in playing women's roles, a tradition that continues undisturbed in Japanese *kabuki*.

CREDITS

Cover: Photographer unknown; from the Hawaii State Archives.

Frontispiece: Photographer unknown; from the Hawaii State Archives.

6 From the Hawaii State Archives.

8 Photographer unknown; from the Bernice Pauahi Bishop Museum.

12–13 Allan Seiden.

14 Frank Salmoiraghi.

16 Brett Uprichard.

17 Allan Seiden.

18 Frank Salmoiraghi.

19 Allan Seiden.

20–21 Joe Carini.

22 Warren Bolster.

23 Greg Vaughn.

24 Joe Carini.

25 Val Kim.

26 Hideki Iwanaga, ca. 1920; from the Alexander & Baldwin Sugar Museum, Puunene, Maui.

27 Christian Hedemann; from the Bernice Pauahi Bishop Museum.

28 Photographer unknown; from the Bernice Pauahi Bishop Museum.

31 Hideki Iwanaga; from the Alexander & Baldwin Sugar Museum, Puunene, Maui.

33 Acrylic painting by Guy Buffet.

34–35 Frank Salmoiraghi.

37 Morito Koga photo; from the Bernice Pauahi Bishop Museum.

38 Frank Salmoiraghi.

40 Shuzo Uemoto.

41 Movie still from the Japanese silent film *Father*, 1924, directed by Yasujiro Shimazu.

42–43 Usaku Teragawachi; from the Bernice Pauahi Bishop Museum.

44 Usaku Teragawachi; from the Bernice Pauahi Bishop Museum.

47 Usaku Teragawachi; from the Bernice Pauahi Bishop Museum.

48–53 Usaku Teragawachi; from the Bernice Pauahi Bishop Museum.

54–55 From the Hawaii State Archives.

56 From the Hawaii State Archives.

59 From the Hawaii State Archives.

60–61 From the U.S. Army Museum of Hawaii.

62–63 Cartoon by Corky Trinidad.

64 Roy Ito; from the *Honolulu Advertiser*.

67 Greg Vaughn.

68 Greg Vaughn.

71 Photo courtesy of the National Aeronautics and Space Administration (NASA).

73 Joe Carini.

75 Frank Salmoiraghi.

76–77 Woodblock engraving by Isami Doi.

78 Woodblock engraving by Isami Doi.

81 Welded metal sculpture by Satoru Abe.

82 Oil painting by Tadashi Sato.

83 Watercolor painting by Charles Higa.

84 Watercolor painting by Paul Nagano.

85 Watercolor painting by Hiroki Morinoue.

86 Oil painting by Tetsuo Ochikubo.

87 Watercolor painting by Myles Tanaka.

88 Photoetching by John Morita.

89 Lithograph by Wayne Muromoto.

90 Acrylic and watercolor painting by Brian Isobe.

91 Oil painting by Shige Yamada.

92 Construction by Reiko Mochinaga Brandon.

93 Tapestry by Akiko Kotani.

94 Ceramic by Randy Hokushin.

95 Ceramic by David Kuraoka.

96 Ceramic by Nina Hagiwara Peterson.

97 Sculpture by Marie Kodama.

98 Sculpture by Mamoru Sato.

99 Sculpture by Bumpei Akaji.

100–101 Sculpture by Douglas Doi.

103 Ceramic by Toshiko Takaezu.

104–105 Ihara photo.

107 Frank Salmoiraghi.

109 Frank Salmoiraghi.

110 Shuzo Uemoto.

112–113 Shuzo Uemoto.

114–115 Shuzo Uemoto.

116–117 Stan Tomita.

118–119 Stan Tomita.

120–121 Stan Tomita.

122–123 Paul Kodama.

124–125 Frank Salmoiraghi.

126–127 Gaylord Kubota.

128 Dana Edmunds.

130 Greg Vaughn.

131 Gaylord Kubota.

132 Frank Salmoiraghi.

133 Wayne Levin.

134 Michael Young.

135 Carl Shaneff.

136–137 Frank Salmoiraghi.

138 Doug Peebles.

139 Greg Vaughn.

140 Frank Salmoiraghi.

143 Greg Vaughn.

144 Pen and ink drawing by Maile Yawata.

146 Photographer unknown; from the Bernice Pauahi Bishop Museum.

149 Photographer unknown; from the Bernice Pauahi Bishop Museum.

154 Frank Salmoiraghi.

158 Photographer unknown; from the Alexander & Baldwin Sugar Museum, Puunene, Maui.

Back Cover: J. J. Williams; from the Hawaii State Archives.

ACKNOWLEDGEMENTS

The parallels between the *Tenjiku* sought by the *Gannenmono* of 1868 and the publishing excellence sought by the many creators of this book are striking indeed. Both followed an arduous path to produce the history and now this account of Japanese life in Hawaii. As in all worthy efforts of this scope, this book required a total commitment by all parties involved. Our sincere gratitude, therefore, is extended to all persons who participated in this effort. *Kanyaku Imin, A Hundred Years of Japanese Life in Hawaii,* was nurtured by the energies of many island artists, journalists and businessmen who truly care about this unique period in Hawaii's history.

Initially, it would not have been possible to produce this book without the patience, vision and unrelenting persistence of editorial director Leonard Lueras. His ability to quickly consolidate the thoughts and perspectives of a complex team of creative people was commendable. He and Kunio Hayashi, art director of Media Five Ltd, Honolulu's prestigious design corporation, have produced a book of lasting value.

Additionally, it was great pride in Hawaii's unique Japanese community that was a major motivating factor in this work, and for this much *aloha* and thanks is due to Lionel Tokioka, chairman of the International Savings and Loan Association Ltd, who provided general financial support and encouragement; Sam Okinaga, chairman of KHNL-TV's management committee, who carefully steered this book from the idea stage into reality; and Rick Blangiardi, the general manager of KHNL-TV, who kept early hopes of producing this book alive, well and enthusiastic. I join these key sponsors in hoping that this book will be a perpetual remembrance of this year's Centennial celebration honoring those Japanese citizens who forged a new homeland here for their children.

Other individuals who contributed immensely and have earned our sincere appreciation include Michael Leineweber, AIA, a principal and vice-president of Media Five Ltd, who provided studio facilities for production work; Nedra Chung, who spent many hours researching, copy-editing and indexing the book; Jay Hartwell, who gave strong editorial support during the book's "deadline" stages; Rene Kitagawa, who worked closely with Lueras and Hayashi on final design matters; and Mary Mitsuda (acting director), Laila and Thurston Twigg-Smith, Fae Yamaguchi and Linda Gué of the Contemporary Arts Center of Hawaii, who made possible the special portfolio on local Japanese artists. Additional thanks also to Mike Einstein, Dana and Ginger Edmunds, Hiromi Hayashi, Ron Hudson, Keiji Kawakami, Ann Kimura, Gaylord Kubota, Jacqueline Langley, Carl Lindquist and Vicki Villaluz, among many others.

Local institutions which participated in this book also deserve a very warm *mahalo*. Among these are the photo archives of the Bernice Pauahi Bishop Museum and the Hawaii State Archives, the Hawaiian Historical Society, the Alexander and Baldwin Sugar Museum, the Japanese Chamber of Commerce, *Winds,* the inflight magazine of Japan Air Lines, Emphasis International and Emphasis Hong Kong Ltd and the University of Hawaii Press, which graciously allowed us to use excerpts from O. A. Bushnell's fine novel *The Stone of Kannon.*

Finally, I would like to thank King Kalakaua and the Japanese people for jointly believing that progress toward ideal human relationships lies in an understanding of our differences and an appreciation of our similarities. Their beliefs and the courageous determination of Hawaii's *Kanyaku Imin* have enriched our lives forever.

—Michael Langley
Project Coordinator